WHAT'S
THE
MESSAGE?

WHAT'S THE MESSAGE?

BIBLE BASICS FOR BUSY PEOPLE

Kevin Sullivan

Paulist Press
New York / Mahwah, NJ

Cover design by Joe Gallagher
Book design by Lynn Else

Library of Congress Cataloging-in-Publication Data
Names: Sullivan, Kevin (Monsignor), author.
Title: What's the message? : Bible basics for busy people / Kevin Sullivan.
Description: New York / Mahwah, NJ : Paulist Press, [2022] | Summary: "This scaled-back Bible is a brief and accessible guide for readers today, whose time and attention are strained by demands of daily life. In a clear and relevant manner, What's the Message? offers a frank approach for religious, nonreligious, and spiritually minded folks from all religions (or none) to get to know the Bible's big themes. The focus on key biblical passages with connected reflections carves a pathway to the heart of the Bible"—Provided by publisher.
Identifiers: LCCN 2021023958 (print) | LCCN 2021023959 (ebook) | ISBN 9780809155224 (paperback) | ISBN 9781587689178 (ebook)
Subjects: LCSH: Bible—Introductions.
Classification: LCC BS475.3 .S83 2022 (print) | LCC BS475.3 (ebook) | DDC 220.6/1—dc23
LC record available at https://lccn.loc.gov/2021023958
LC ebook record available at https://lccn.loc.gov/2021023959

ISBN 978-0-8091-5522-4 (paperback)
ISBN 978-1-58768-917-8 (e-book)

Published by Paulist Press
997 Macarthur Boulevard
Mahwah, New Jersey 07430
www.paulistpress.com

Printed and bound in the
United States of America

Deborah Darrell
March 11, 1965 – December 30, 2014
My friend who agitated the scheme for the book
and
John P. Meier
Who has taught thousands much about the Bible,
including me—I'm grateful to have learned a little

"I believe the Bible is the best gift God has ever given to man."

—Abraham Lincoln

CONTENTS

Contents

Contents

Contents

PREFACE
Just the FAQs

TL;DR is text for "too long; didn't read." That's what many of you might be thinking about the Bible: The (*Very*) Big Book. I've thought it myself. That's why I'm breaking it down in *What's the Message?* for all the other attention-challenged readers out there. Let me answer several legit FAQs about what I'm attempting to do.

1. WHAT KIND OF BOOK ABOUT THE BIBLE IS THIS?

It's *not* a book *about* the Bible. It's a really, really short "version" of the Bible that presents twenty-five key passages, organizes them into ten themes, and makes the outrageous claim that this captures the Bible's basic message—in brief.

2. WHY ONLY THE "BASICS"? WHAT ABOUT THE *WHOLE THING*?

The whole Bible is pretty big, some 800,000 words— TL;DR. Sorry, God, but it's true. And its message is too important to let length be an obstacle. So, for me and my attention-challenged friends and everyone of nanosecond, sound bite, or Twitter ilk, here's my humble attempt at the Cliff Notes or SparkNotes version.

3. AM I BIASED IN PICKING THE CORE PASSAGES?

Yes, guilty! I fear this book will likely offend some faith-filled pious folks and, of course, the scholars. But I have hung out with the Bible for more than a few decades—studying, listening, and preaching. Here, I'm considering passages that give me a clue about the Big Book's core message. I have a hunch they'll do that for you, as they have for many others. A few extras are thrown in for those who want more. Disclaimer: Sometimes I've skipped a verse or grafted on a verse from a different book. (Apologies upfront!)

4. WHAT ABOUT THE SELF-HELP TIPS?

I'm striving to be a better person, but I don't like being told what to do, the approach religion has mastered. And while I like to figure things out for myself, I can always use some tips. I've shared "Ponderings" after each Bible passage, with the hope they prompt your own reflections. **Spoiler Alert:** Although the Bible is the best self-help book of all time, that still doesn't mean I'm trying to make sense of things without God's help.

5. ARE THESE HOLY TIPS ON HOW TO MAKE SURE WE GET TO HEAVEN?

No way! Others can do that much better. These tips focus on living better here and now on earth. They are relevant to the messy, chaotic, and hopeful roads we journey on each day. Hopefully, they include a bit of heavenly wisdom.

6. WHAT ABOUT THE STYLE?

I have a confession to make. I sometimes get bored and distracted by the usual style of spiritual writing. These tips are different and maybe even a little irreverent, with the hope they open up the Bible's ancient wisdom for our times.

7. WHO IS THIS BOOK FOR?

Believers, nonbelievers, the attention-challenged, self-helpers, anyone very (or maybe even too) familiar with the Bible, and those who don't know much about it—for ALL Y'ALL open to learning more about yourselves, relationships...and, of course, more about God.

I hear some asking, "Can you get on with it?" You're tired of these Q&As? NUFF SAID. Let's get to know God and ourselves better. It's a potent partnership. Enjoy and share what you learn.

ACKNOWLEDGMENTS

This short book has been developed over five years, with stops and starts for several reasons. During that time, I have spoken with and listened to many people whose insights have guided and shaped the book. Some have been quite helpful with specific aspects. Lest I omit anyone, I will not mention names. They know who they are, and I say to all, "Thank you."

PART 1

THE STORYLINE

Basic Passages & Ponderings

INTRODUCTION
The Bible's Basic Storyline

CREATION

In the beginning, God created Mother Earth as good, and us as very good, putting his very own stamp (image) on us.

A CHOSEN PEOPLE: ABRAHAM, MOSES, AND THE PROMISED LAND

Then he called Abram/Abraham to abandon his homeland, believe God's promise to make his descendants into a great nation—God's chosen people, the Jews, and even more, to bless all nations. But the path was jarring. The Jews wound up as slaves in Egypt...for a long time.

Next, God called a reluctant and flawed Moses to be their liberator and chaperone to the promised land. Moses taught (Ten Commandments), scolded (golden calf incident), and interceded (manna from heaven) for the Israelites for forty Bible years or so until they got to the promised land. (**Spoiler Alert:** Moses didn't get to go in. He messed up big time!)

After that, the Jews became a "real" nation with kings, armies, a treasury, and a temple. Sometimes it went well and sometimes not so much. They got conquered and dragged off into exile for a while. The prophets, God's special agents, told the people two Big Messages: God was going to send them a Messiah and they couldn't keep God's message for themselves. They had to enlighten non-Jews.

THE BIRTH

Then came the Big Moment: "Team God" sent one of their own, Jesus, whose mom, Mary, was a young Jewish girl from Nazareth, to preach, heal, feed, and save (aka the Messiah, the Christ).

THE MESSAGE AND TALKING TO GOD

Jesus attracted attention and committed followers. Crowds of people listened to his message and stories. He said old commonsense stuff, new inspiring stuff, and also outrageous stuff about how tight he was with God. Jesus even called God "Dad" and told his followers to do the same when they prayed. Love, mercy, and service were Jesus's answers to a lot of questions and puzzled looks he got.

THE MEMORIAL MEAL

Knowing he was near the end, Jesus instituted a memorial meal for his followers to remember and be nourished by him until he came back.

DEATH

The political and religious establishments got nervous and plotted against Jesus. On a Friday afternoon in broad daylight, during the Jewish festival of Passover, they killed him on a cross.

NEW LIFE

Everybody thought it was over, including his friends, so they hid from fear. But his Father in heaven had in mind a better ending: on the third day, Sunday, Jesus was raised up to new life in history's all-time game changer!

Then Jesus appeared for forty days to make sure his followers got that he was not dead but alive. After that, Jesus ascended back to heaven, tasking his followers to spread the Big Message with the help of the Holy Spirit.

THE HOLY SPIRIT

As promised, Jesus and his dad sent "No. 3" in the family: the lesser known but dynamite Holy Spirit, who was to strengthen, advocate for, and advise Jesus's motley followers until Jesus's return on the last day. That same Spirit is still hanging out to help us deal with the good, the bad, and the ugly along our earthly trek.

A NEW HEAVEN & A NEW EARTH

When Jesus comes again, it will all be over and all will be good. No more tears, no crying, only peace, joy, and love forever! No contingencies! The ultimate perfect ending!

THE GOOD BOOK:
A GOOD STORY ABOUT GOOD STUFF

That's the Bible's basic storyline crunched from the Big Book's 800,000 words, which tell about:

- God and his Chosen People
- How to get in touch with God
- How Jesus wants his followers to live
- The Presence and Power of the Spirit
- The endgame of peace, happiness, and love

Funny how this good stuff written thousands of years ago is still on target and worth getting to know. That's why I'm giving you the Bible Basics in twenty-five key passages, with self-help reflection tips, "ponderings," to explore more about yourself, your relationships, and God.

1

LET'S START AT THE BEGINNING

Genesis 1:1–31

Creation

In the beginning when God created the heavens and the earth, the earth was a formless void and darkness covered the face of the deep, while a wind from God swept over the face of the waters. Then God said, "Let there be light"; and there was light. And God saw that the light was good; and God separated the light from the darkness. God called the light Day, and the darkness he called Night. And there was evening and there was morning, the first day.

And God said, "Let there be a dome in the midst of the waters, and let it separate the waters from the waters." So, God made the dome and separated the waters that were under the dome from the waters that were above the dome. And it was so.

God called the dome Sky. And there was evening and there was morning, the second day.

And God said, "Let the waters under the sky be gathered together into one place, and let the dry land appear." And it was so. God called the dry land Earth, and the waters that were gathered together he called Seas. And God saw that it was good. Then God said, "Let the earth put forth vegetation: plants yielding seed, and fruit trees of every kind on earth that bear fruit with the seed in it." And it was so. The earth brought forth vegetation: plants yielding seed of every kind, and trees of every kind bearing fruit with the seed in it. And God saw that it was good. And there was evening and there was morning, the third day.

And God said, "Let there be lights in the dome of the sky to separate the day from the night; and let them be for signs and for seasons and for days and years, and let them be lights in the dome of the sky to give light upon the earth." And it was so. God made the two great lights—the greater light to rule the day and the lesser light to rule the night—and the stars. God set them in the dome of the sky to give light upon the earth, to rule over the day and over the night, and to separate the light from the darkness. And God saw that it was good. And there was evening and there was morning, the fourth day.

And God said, "Let the waters bring forth swarms of living creatures, and let birds fly above the earth across the dome of the sky." So, God created the great sea monsters and every living creature that moves, of every kind, with which the waters swarm, and every winged bird of every kind. And God saw that it was good. God blessed them, saying, "Be fruitful and multiply and fill the waters in the seas, and let birds multiply on the earth." And there was evening and there was morning, the fifth day.

And God said, "Let the earth bring forth living creatures of every kind: cattle and creeping things and wild animals of the earth of every kind." And it was so. God made the wild animals of the earth of every kind, and the cattle of every kind, and everything that creeps upon the ground of every kind. And God saw that it was good.

Then God said, "Let us make humankind in our image, according to our likeness; and let them have dominion over the fish of the sea, and over the birds of the air, and over the cattle, and over all the wild animals of the earth, and over every creeping thing that creeps upon the earth."

So, God created humankind in his image, in the image of God he created them; male and female he created them.

God blessed them, and God said to them, "Be fruitful and multiply, and fill the earth and subdue it; and have dominion over the fish of the sea and over the birds of the air and over every living thing that moves upon the earth." God said, "See, I have given you every plant yielding seed that is upon the face of all the earth, and every tree with seed in its fruit; you shall have them for food. And to every beast of the earth, and to every bird of the air, and to everything that creeps on the earth, everything that has the breath of life, I have given every green plant for food." And it was so. God saw everything that he had made, and indeed, it was very good.

And there was evening and there was morning, the sixth day.

Ponderings

When my attention-challenges are really kicking in, this is my "go-to" passage. God, you, me, and all creation—together in one section—that's efficiency!

I begin with the climax: God made me; and God made me in his image and likeness; and it's "very good." I am God-like and good. Wow! Let me take a moment to take this in. (But let's not get too big a head—I am not God and not perfect. Can't forget this big difference.) And it's not only about me. God not only made me, but he made you and all of us—every single human being, every man, every woman, in his image and likeness. That's a pretty big deal.

Then I think about how God made the whole world and everything in it good, too. It's all tied together because he gave humankind dominion (I prefer "stewardship" or "care") of all Creation. Guess this Go Green thing is not a contemporary brainchild. It was in God's mind from the beginning. The same Creator made Mother Earth and all the critters who inhabit it. Be good to your Mother! It's taken us human beings more than a few years to catch on.

Like I said, it's almost all here and I could meditate on this passage for a long time.

A Few Additional Thoughts

This passage touches on some very sensitive, serious, and yes, divisive issues that we are dealing with in the twenty-first century: marriage and family, gender roles and equality, sexual orientation and identity, evolution, ecology, fauna and flora, and so on. These are real issues we need to deal with, but please don't get distracted or disappointed that this passage doesn't resolve them. Don't burden this chapter of the Bible, composed millennia ago with the task of providing detailed answers to specific contemporary questions. They're not there. Important values and perspectives, to be sure, and not to be ignored. But don't misuse the Bible: it's neither a debate manual nor a science textbook. If you want to fight about creationism and gender issues, OK, your choice, but use other tools—and please do so respectfully and civilly.

One Final Thought

The darker the times, the more enlightening the story of creation! Spend some time reflecting on the Bible's magnificent opening lines and its central assertion: We humans are God-like, equal, diverse, sacred, social, stewards of creation, and are very good. I'll keep my membership card in the human race.

2

A CHOSEN PEOPLE

Leader Abraham: A People & a Promise

After these things the word of the Lord came to Abram in a vision, "Do not be afraid, Abram, I am your shield; your reward shall be very great." But Abram said, "O Lord God, what will you give me, for I continue childless, and the heir of my house is Eliezer of Damascus?" And Abram said, "You have given me no offspring, and so a slave born in my house is to be my heir." But the word of the Lord came to him, "This man shall not be your heir; no one but your very own issue shall be your heir." He brought him outside and said, "Look toward heaven and count the stars, if you are able to count them." Then he said to him, "So shall your descendants be." And he believed the Lord; and the Lord reckoned it to him as righteousness.

Then he said to him, "I am the Lord who brought you from Ur of the Chaldeans, to give you this land to possess." But he said, "O Lord GOD, how am I to know that I shall possess it?" He said to him, "Bring me a heifer three years old, a female goat three years old, a ram three years old, a turtledove, and a young pigeon." He brought him all these and cut them in two, laying each half over against the other; but he did not cut the birds in two. And when birds of prey came down on the carcasses, Abram drove them away.

As the sun was going down, a deep sleep fell upon Abram, and a deep and terrifying darkness descended upon him. Then the LORD said to Abram, "Know this for certain, that your offspring shall be aliens in a land that is not theirs, and shall be slaves there, and they shall be oppressed for four hundred years; but I will bring judgment on the nation that they serve, and afterward they shall come out with great possessions. As for yourself, you shall go to your ancestors in peace; you shall be buried in a good old age. And they shall come back here in the fourth generation; for the iniquity of the Amorites is not yet complete."

When the sun had gone down and it was dark, a smoking fire pot and a flaming torch passed between these pieces. On that day the LORD made a covenant with Abram, saying, "To your descendants I give this land, from the river of Egypt to the great river, the river Euphrates."

Ponderings

Why did God pick *one* people to be specially chosen and *one* person to be their "founding father?" I'm not sure I would have, and I don't know why God did—seems chancy and maybe even a bit elitist. But if we can cut God a few millennia of slack, we will see that "soon"—according to God's timeline—everybody gets the call.

So God chooses Abram (Father), gives him a name change to Abraham (Father of Many), and tells the seventy-five-year-old "childless one" he is going to have kids and lots and lots of descendants—even more than the stars. And so, the story of Israel begins.

Let's talk about the covenant, the deal, between God and Abraham. God puts on the table the basic terms: change your name, have kids, move to a better neighborhood, your offspring will have great wealth in expansive and fertile territory. (BTW: God didn't hide the deferred gratification part—four hundred years of slavery, huge obstacles.) Abraham's ante in this deal is faith.

So, Abraham gambles away his current life and trusts in the future God sets before him. Because of that, today every Jew, Christian, and Muslim, totaling over 4 billion—more than half the world's population in the twenty-first century—call Abraham our Father in Faith. Not a bad return on investment and legacy for a seventy-five-year-old with a barren wife.

This deal may be a good model for situations in our own lives. We're better off to let God do most of the talking, promising, and working. He is much better at it than we are—and has more to offer. If we can simply make a small effort to trust, it usually works out pretty well, even if it's not quite the epic impact of Abraham. OK, I admit trusting isn't always that simple—whether it's trusting God, another person, or especially myself. But it's worth a try.

Exodus 3:1–22

A Reluctant Moses, an Enigmatic God, and a People Freed

Moses was keeping the flock of his father-in-law Jethro, the priest of Midian; he led his flock beyond the wilderness, and came to Horeb, the mountain of God. There the angel of the LORD appeared to him in a flame of fire out of a bush; he looked, and the bush was blazing, yet it was not consumed. Then Moses said, "I must turn aside and look at this great sight, and see why the bush is not burned up." When the LORD saw that he had turned aside to see, God called to him out of the bush, "Moses, Moses!" And he said, "Here I am." Then he said, "Come no closer! Remove the sandals from your feet, for the place on which you are standing is holy ground." He said further, "I am the God of your father, the God of Abraham, the God of Isaac, and the God of Jacob." And Moses hid his face, for he was afraid to look at God.

Then the LORD said, "I have observed the misery of my people who are in Egypt; I have heard their cry on account of their taskmasters. Indeed, I know their sufferings, and I have come down to deliver them from the Egyptians, and to bring them up out of that land to a good and broad land, a land flowing with milk and honey, to the country of the Canaanites, the Hittites, the Amorites, the Perizzites, the Hivites, and the Jebusites. The cry of the Israelites has now come to me; I have also seen how the Egyptians oppress them. So come, I will send you to Pharaoh to bring my people, the Israelites, out of Egypt."

But Moses said to God, "Who am I that I should go to Pharaoh, and bring the Israelites out of Egypt?" He said, "I will be with you; and this shall be the sign for you that it is I who sent you: when you have brought the people out of Egypt, you shall worship God on this mountain." But Moses said to God, "If I come to the Israelites and say to them, 'The God of your ancestors has sent me to you,' and they ask me, 'What is his name?' what shall I say to them?" God said to Moses, "I AM WHO I AM." He said further, "Thus you shall say to the Israelites, 'I AM has sent me to you.'" God also said to Moses, "Thus you shall say to the Israelites, 'The LORD, the God of your ancestors, the God of Abraham, the God of Isaac, and the God of Jacob, has sent me to you': This is my name forever, and this my title for all generations.

Go and assemble the elders of Israel, and say to them, 'The LORD, the God of your ancestors, the God of Abraham, of Isaac, and of Jacob, has appeared to me, saying: I have given heed to you and to what has been done to you in Egypt. I declare that I will bring you up out of the misery of Egypt, to the land of the Canaanites, the Hittites, the Amorites, the Perizzites, the Hivites, and the Jebusites, a land flowing with milk and honey.' They will listen to your voice; and you and the elders of Israel shall go to the king of Egypt and say to him, 'The LORD, the God of the Hebrews, has met with us; let us now go a three days' journey into the wilderness, so that we may sacrifice to the LORD our

God.' I know, however, that the king of Egypt will not let you go unless compelled by a mighty hand. So I will stretch out my hand and strike Egypt with all my wonders that I will perform in it; after that he will let you go. I will bring this people into such favor with the Egyptians that, when you go, you will not go empty-handed; each woman shall ask her neighbor and any woman living in the neighbor's house for jewelry of silver and of gold, and clothing, and you shall put them on your sons and on your daughters; and so you shall plunder the Egyptians."

Ponderings

God chooses strange leaders. Moses: abandoned at birth by his mother, raised in an alien home, murderer, fugitive, arguer with God, a hesitant liberator. (Preview: It doesn't get much better when we learn about Jesus's draft choices!)

Yet it *is* Moses whom God calls to the burning bush to be sent to free his people from the oppression of Egypt and lead them to the land flowing with milk and honey.

Moses doesn't accept this assignment eagerly and seeks to negotiate for power over God by asking God's name. At that time—and to a lesser extent even now—if you knew somebody's name you had some control over that person. Sound familiar? The tendency to want to control still runs deep in us.

God's cryptic response, "I AM WHO I AM" (and its various alternate translations), is in the running for the most written about verse in the Bible. So, with due deference to the millions of scholarly words of commentary, let me put it my way: God does not avoid the question, rather he answers it very clearly and directly, and in a way that frustrates and guts Moses's—and all of humankind's—chutzpah in trying to control God. Here's my translation of God's response to Moses, and to us: "I am who I will be, and I am with you as I am—not as you want. Let me be clear about the meaning of my name: I am the one uncontrollable by humankind but always present to you." So, Moses goes on the way God sent him. Then comes the crossing of the Red Sea, the long journey in the desert, the giving of the Ten Commandments, and the entrance into the promised land.

DEUTERONOMY 5:1–22

A Saving God with a Few Demands

Moses convened all Israel, and said to them:

Hear, O Israel, the statutes and ordinances that I am addressing to you today; you shall learn them and observe them diligently. The LORD our God made a covenant with us at Horeb. Not with our ancestors did the LORD make this covenant, but with us, who are all of us here alive today. The LORD spoke with you face to face at the mountain, out of the fire. (At that time I was standing between the LORD and you to declare to you the words of the LORD; for you were afraid because of the fire and did not go up the mountain.) And he said:

I am the LORD your God, who brought you out of the land of Egypt, out of the house of slavery; you shall have no other gods before me.

You shall not make for yourself an idol, whether in the form of anything that is in heaven above, or that is on the earth beneath, or that is in the water under the earth. You shall not bow down to them or worship them; for I the LORD your God am a jealous God, punishing children for the iniquity of parents, to the third and fourth generation of those who reject me, but showing steadfast love to the thousandth generation of those who love me and keep my commandments.

You shall not make wrongful use of the name of the LORD your God, for the LORD will not acquit anyone who misuses his name.

Observe the sabbath day and keep it holy, as the LORD your God commanded you. Six days you shall labor and do all your work. But the seventh day is a sabbath to the LORD your God; you shall not do any work—you, or your son or your daughter, or your male or female slave, or your ox or your donkey, or any of your livestock, or the resident alien in your towns, so that your male and female slave may rest as well as you. Remember that you were a slave in the land of Egypt, and the LORD your God brought you out from there with a mighty hand and an outstretched arm; therefore the LORD your God commanded you to keep the sabbath day.

Honor your father and your mother, as the LORD your God commanded you, so that your days may be long and that it may go well with you in the land that the LORD your God is giving you.

You shall not murder.

Neither shall you commit adultery.

Neither shall you steal.

Neither shall you bear false witness against your neighbor.

Neither shall you covet your neighbor's wife.

Neither shall you desire your neighbor's house, or field, or male or female slave, or ox, or donkey, or anything that belongs to your neighbor.

These words the LORD spoke with a loud voice to your whole assembly at the mountain, out of the fire, the cloud, and the thick darkness, and he added no more. He wrote them on two stone tablets, and gave them to me.

Ponderings

Yes, the Ten Commandments, but they don't stand alone. God's clever in delivering his expectations. First, he reminds his people how bad they had it as slaves in Egypt, and who liberated them. A not-so-subtle reminder there's no free lunch! "Now here's ten things I want you to do." Most of them are common sense, and by now we've heard most of them over and over again. A few (the first three) are about how we treat God and most (the final seven) are about how we treat one another. Note to self: God seems really concerned that we do right by one another, maybe even more so than focusing on him...by a margin of seven to three.

The first deal with God—worship only one God, don't curse or use God's name too casually or hypocritically, keep the Sabbath. The second group deals with others in the neighborhood: don't kill them, don't steal from them (or even want to), don't fool around with their spouses (or even want to), don't lie to them, be good to Mom and Dad. Pretty straightforward and basic. They don't seem to be an outrageous ask for being liberated from the four hundred years of slavery in Egypt. Taken together these seem to be a pretty reasonable price for the gift of being saved.

(Sneak peek: Do you think this first part [God], second part [neighbors] framework might be a trailer for the "two great love commandments"?)

Sourced from a distant desert a long time ago, these ten dictums still can stir some rewarding contemporary reflections.

Let's take just one. How are we doing about "keeping the Sabbath"? Worshiping, praying, and going to church is one part, but what about "rest"? Don't all the contemporary self-help and wellness gurus talk about "disconnecting"? Are iPhones, tablets, Twitter, and Instagram also entitled to Sabbath rest? Was Moses way ahead of his time in pushing Sabbath rest? Why don't you think about the other nine? I'll bet they might even work today if we want to ask God to free us from the oppressions, addictions, and obsessions that enslave us. Sorry to get too heavy—just a thought.

Ezekiel 36:16–28

Forgiveness, Renewal, and God's Nearness

The word of the LORD came to me: Mortal, when the house of Israel lived on their own soil, they defiled it with their ways and their deeds; their conduct in my sight was like the uncleanness of a woman in her menstrual period. So I poured out my wrath upon them for the blood that they had shed upon the land, and for the idols with which they had defiled it. I scattered them among the nations, and they were dispersed through the countries; in accordance with their conduct and their deeds I judged them. But when they came to the nations, wherever they came, they profaned my holy name, in that it was said of them, "These are the people of the LORD, and yet they had to go out of his land." But I had concern for my holy name, which the house of Israel had profaned among the nations to which they came.

Therefore say to the house of Israel, Thus says the Lord GOD: It is not for your sake, O house of

Israel, that I am about to act, but for the sake of my holy name, which you have profaned among the nations to which you came. I will sanctify my great name, which has been profaned among the nations, and which you have profaned among them; and the nations shall know that I am the LORD, says the Lord GOD, when through you I display my holiness before their eyes. I will take you from the nations, and gather you from all the countries, and bring you into your own land. I will sprinkle clean water upon you, and you shall be clean from all your unclean-ness, and from all your idols I will cleanse you. A new heart I will give you, and a new spirit I will put within you; and I will remove from your body the heart of stone and give you a heart of flesh. I will put my spirit within you, and make you follow my statutes and be careful to observe my ordinances. Then you shall live in the land that I gave to your ancestors; and you shall be my people, and I will be your God.

Ponderings

God's no pushover, but he can't help saving his people (us). They (we) act badly. They were unfaithful and ungrate-ful. And God says, "You better shape up."

"And if that doesn't work, I'll change you from the inside out: a new heart, a new spirit—and then you'll get it right." Now that's the ultimate "extreme makeover" designed by the Creator. I guess God's got a stake in us since "in the begin-ning," we've got his image and likeness within us.

What a wonderful God who says, "I'm your God"—even when we fail. So, I'll make it even. I'm willing to call him "*My*

God," even when he fails. *Oops!* I'm not supposed to say that. OK, let me rephrase that. I'm still claiming him as my God even when I don't get what he's up to, and so I feel like he is failing me. Sorry, God, but that's the way I feel sometimes. But even then, I'll still call you, "*My* God."

3

GOD BECOMES HUMAN

LUKE 2:1–14

The Down-to-Earth Story: Jesus Is Born in Bethlehem

In those days a decree went out from Emperor Augustus that all the world should be registered. This was the first registration and was taken while Quirinius was governor of Syria. All went to their own towns to be registered. Joseph also went from the town of Nazareth in Galilee to Judea, to the city of David called Bethlehem, because he was descended from the house and family of David. He went to be registered with Mary, to whom he was engaged and who was expecting a child. While they were there, the time came for her to deliver her child. And she gave birth to her firstborn son and wrapped him in bands of cloth, and laid him in a manger because there was no place for them in the inn.

In that region there were shepherds living in the fields, keeping watch over their flock by night.

Then an angel of the Lord stood before them, and the glory of the Lord shone around them, and they were terrified. But the angel said to them, "Do not be afraid; for see—I am bringing you good news of great joy for all the people: to you is born this day in the city of David a Savior, who is the Messiah, the Lord. This will be a sign for you: you will find a child wrapped in bands of cloth and lying in a manger." And suddenly there was with the angel a multitude of the heavenly host, praising God and saying,

"Glory to God in the highest heaven,
and on earth peace among those whom he favors!"

Ponderings

Mary's manger-born baby son will one day be touted as King of the Jews by Pontius Pilate's etching on his cross, and Christ, King of the Universe, by his followers throughout the world.

The beginning is a different kind of royal procession: an eighty-mile trek by Joseph and eight-month-pregnant Mary from the lowlands of Nazareth up to the hills of Judea, ending in crowded "no vacancy" Bethlehem! While there, Mary goes into labor and Jesus is born in a feeding trough. Where's the twenty-four-hour news coverage; where's the easel in front of the palace? No paparazzi, no tweets, no posts, no Tik Tok. Can it be real? Can it be all that important?!

Ah, but God's messenger, a single angel, appears to break the news and scares the bejesus (I guess literally!) out of a few shepherds in the fields. The angel gives them the "exclusive" on *the* greatest message of all time—the Savior, Christ the Lord, is born today in Bethlehem!

Finally, in case the shepherds are a little dense, the cavalry shows up—a legion of angels—to trumpet the meaning of this news: "Glory to God in the highest heaven, and on earth peace among those whom he favors."

Give me a moment to take in this: God gets praised and we get peace. Wow and...*wow*! I'm taking this deal!

What kind of God is it that uses such ordinary human matters to change the world in extraordinary ways? A simple faith-filled couple, Mary and Joseph, faces an unexpected and unimaginable conception. A census mandate forces a late-term journey to Joseph's crowded hometown of Bethlehem. A manger becomes a crib. Shepherds doing their regular jobs and minding their own business are the first to get news. Maybe I should pay more attention to the ordinary of my own time and space. Is it possible, amid the din, that I'll hear of a message that gives God some praise and me some peace. I'm betting on it. Glory to God in heaven and peace to his people on earth! Wow and *wow*!

John 1:1–14

The Heady Version

In the beginning was the Word, and the Word was with God, and the Word was God. He was in the beginning with God. All things came into being through him, and without him not one thing came into being. What has come into being in him was life, and the life was the light of all people. The light shines in the darkness, and the darkness did not overcome it.

There was a man sent from God, whose name was John. He came as a witness to testify to the light, so that all might believe through him. He himself was not the light, but he came to testify to the light. The true light, which enlightens everyone, was coming into the world.

He was in the world, and the world came into being through him; yet the world did not know him. He came to what was his own, and his own people did not accept him. But to all who received him, who believed in his name, he gave power to become children of God, who were born, not of blood or of the will of the flesh or of the will of man, but of God.

And the Word became flesh and lived among us, and we have seen his glory, the glory as of a father's only son, full of grace and truth.

Ponderings

In case you didn't recognize it, this is the intellectual version of the Christmas story with a historical intro. Please cut me an extra dose of slack here with my attempt to reduce to bare bones some pretty dense and nuanced verses. To keep it focused, I'm *not* going to offer any tips on John the Baptist and the acceptance or nonacceptance of Jesus, but know that they are definitively worth reflecting on.

Let's begin. First hint, substitute "Jesus" for "the Word" and you'll get most of it. Jesus hung out with God, his father, from the beginning, and, through him, Dad made it all. Without them, *nothing*! Quite a universe-wide construction monopoly for this dynamic duo. (No antitrust laws then!)

Then, after a while—a few millennia or so—Jesus, aka "the Word," aka God, became human. Yup, was born as a baby in the flesh. (Review Luke's version above for more details.) And he lived among us for a few years.

This is heady stuff: *One* God for the whole universe was hard enough at the time Israel was establishing itself, and quite countercultural. Now we have to figure out Team God: Father & Son, Inc. (No, I haven't forgotten about the Holy Spirit. We'll get there shortly, one step at a time.)

If you are confused, relax. The bad news: We will never completely understand this God thing. And forget about solving it! The good news: We don't have to. Let's enjoy the part of the mystery we grasp for today, and tomorrow we hope for another insight and then rejoice in that new gift. Let's celebrate this wonderfully tight, intimate, loving relationship between the Father and Son. So, let's rejoice in the closeness and collaboration between Father God and Son God. Sadly, we see too many human examples of the opposite. Will you pray with me and celebrate greater intimacy for human fathers and human sons?

Let's revel that Team God sent one of its players to take on human flesh and stay with us on earth for a while. (Dear Santa: Please bring me a time machine for Christmas so I can actually touch and see Jesus in the flesh.)

Let's not sell short what this means. In seeing Jesus in our human flesh, we get to see God's glory. And furthermore, we get to experience grace, God's presence, and truth!

Pretty deep—even with my bare-bones thoughts. Don't get me wrong, I like the "manger story"—so down-to-earth. But this version of Team God, Creation, and God becoming human is really something else. Don't worry, my Christmas cards will still be Bethlehem-themed. But my prayers and thoughts spend more time grappling with John's heady version. It's worth a few minutes...actually, a lifetime of reflection.

4

WHAT'S THE MESSAGE?

MATTHEW 22:34–40 (PLUS LUKE 10:28)*

Love God, Love Neighbor

When the Pharisees heard that he had silenced the Sadducees, they gathered together, and one of them, a lawyer, asked him a question to test him. "Teacher, which commandment in the law is the greatest?" He said to him, "'You shall love the Lord your God with all your heart, and with all your soul, and with all your mind.' This is the greatest and first commandment. And a second is like it: 'You shall love your neighbor as yourself.' On these two commandments hang all the law and the prophets." And he said to him, "You have given the right answer; do this, and you will live."

---

* Some might be asking why I stuck a verse from Luke's Gospel onto Matthew's passage. (If you are not one of them, just skip over this next paragraph.) Not to get too technical: Sometimes the Gospels, particularly Matthew, Luke, and Mark, cover the same ground but add or subtract a few details and give you their own take on the core message. Luke's add-on in verse 10:28 is pretty important: "do it and you shall live." So, I grafted it onto Matt's version. Guilty. Doing this is a real "no, no" to true Bible geeks, but they are probably mad at me anyway—for this whole book.

Ponderings

Love God and love your neighbor—less characters than a tweet—sums up the Bible's whole message. That's certainly the answer to this attention-challenged person's prayer. Thank you, God! All in only two easy-to-remember big commandments! Short and sweet, and far from the very (too) complicated way that we religious types sometimes make this God thing. I like when Jesus makes it simple and straightforward like this.

Let me share something from my own family that captures this. My aunt went to Catholic schools. She knew all the correct names for Catholic Mass vestments and the proper explanation for many other parts of the Catholic faith. My father went to public school. He always said his sister knew so much more about her religion than he did. He said he didn't know much. I beg to differ. I observed my dad; here's the little he knew about religion: Be good to people, help those who have less, and pray to God. I'm thinking Jesus would agree that my dad knew quite a bit about his religion—and especially the most important parts.

So, pair these two big commandment verses (love God, love neighbor) with the story of Creation from Genesis (everybody is made of God's image and likeness), and you have a veto-proof, super majority of the message. If you follow them, Jesus says you'll live, and that doesn't mean waiting until heaven to live. If we keep these two biggies, we'll have a good run living well on this earth and even a better life forever in heaven.

Spoiler Alert! Easy to say, not so easy to do. Some days I have a hard time figuring out how to love my neighbor as myself. I am complicated, my neighbor is complicated too, and life is complicated, but it is much better having a clear important goal even if the road is foggy, bumpy, and winding. Let's not stop trying. Even when we get it only partially right, it's well worth it for our neighbors and ourselves

Luke 10:29–37

Who Is My Neighbor?—Surprise!

But wanting to justify himself, he asked Jesus, "And who is my neighbor?" Jesus replied, "A man was going down from Jerusalem to Jericho, and fell into the hands of robbers, who stripped him, beat him, and went away, leaving him half dead. Now by chance a priest was going down that road; and when he saw him, he passed by on the other side. So likewise a Levite, when he came to the place and saw him, passed by on the other side. But a Samaritan while traveling came near him; and when he saw him, he was moved with pity. He went to him and bandaged his wounds, having poured oil and wine on them. Then he put him on his own animal, brought him to an inn, and took care of him. The next day he took out two denarii, gave them to the innkeeper, and said, "Take care of him; and when I come back, I will repay you whatever more you spend." Which of these three, do you think, was a neighbor to the man who fell into the hands of the robbers?" He said, "The one who showed him mercy." Jesus said to him, "Go and do likewise."

Ponderings

Great follow-up question to the commandment to love your neighbor! Who *is* my neighbor? Jesus's answer is not a sentence but the elongated story of the Good Samaritan. If there were a biblical quiz show and the category was "best known and least lived," the Good Samaritan would be in the running for the award.

Now, the easy-to-remember "love commandments" get dicey—and demanding—far beyond common sense and Hallmark or e-card sweetness. We've got the summary message: "Love your neighbor." But surprise! How broadly Jesus now defines neighbor—it includes those who hate me. The Hatfields (read "Reds") are neighbors to the McCoys (read "Blues") and are supposed to do good by each other.

The neighbor is the beat-up stranger from an enemy gang; the refugee fleeing persecution from a hostile country; the unstable homeless guy outside a train station, office building, or church. He or she is the neighbor you and I've got to love like ourselves, even when it's inconvenient or makes me change my plans and forces me to get personally involved. I might even have to touch, which can be messy, dirty, and smelly. How much more challenging is this during the COVID-19 pandemic era (when this book came out)? This "Jesus love thing" is easy to say; but to do—not so much. As with a number of parts of the Bible, God's got a few ideas that make us squirm. This is one of them.

Two other points for pondering:

It's the hated enemy, the Samaritan, who actually acts neighborly and fulfills the commandment. Surprise, shock, yes—certainly to Jesus's audience. Well maybe I can learn something from my "enemies," people I've written off or who are different. Could a Muslim possibly exemplify Christian love? Is it possible that a protester shows a police officer an example of neighborly love? Is it possible that a conservative might have something to teach a liberal, and vice versa?

Could the family of a murdered black teenager be a transformative example of forgiveness and reconciliation to groups more than a little stained with racism?

Don't make excuses when the Church or religious leaders mess up and do bad things or are insensitive. (Substitute bishops, priests, rabbis, and imams for the Levite & priests in the story.)

It's OK to be mad, disappointed, angry, and feel betrayed! But don't let it fester and paralyze you. Go out and love your neighbor as yourself—bind up wounds, help a neighbor in distress. (For other tips, check out chapter 9, MATTHEW 25:31–46, "The Final Exam.")

JOHN 13:2–15

Washing the Disciples' Feet—You, Too!

The devil had already put it into the heart of Judas son of Simon Iscariot to betray him. And during supper Jesus, knowing that the Father had given all things into his hands, and that he had come from God and was going to God, got up from the table, took off his outer robe, and tied a towel around himself. Then he poured water into a basin and began to wash the disciples' feet and to wipe them with the towel that was tied around him. He came to Simon Peter, who said to him, "Lord, are you going to wash my feet?" Jesus answered, "You do not know now what I am doing, but later you will understand." Peter said to him, "You will never wash my feet." Jesus answered, "Unless I wash you, you have no share with me." Simon Peter said to him, "Lord, not my feet only but also my hands and my head!" Jesus said to him, "One who has bathed does not need to wash, except for the feet, but is entirely clean. And you are clean, though not all of you." For he knew who was to betray him; for this reason he said, "Not all of you are clean."

After he had washed their feet, had put on his robe, and had returned to the table, he said to them, "Do you know what I have done to you? You call me Teacher and Lord—and you are right, for that is what I am. So, if I, your Lord and Teacher, have washed your feet, you also ought to wash one another's feet. For I have set you an example, that you also should do as I have done to you."

Ponderings

Here Jesus turns things upside down—again. The Lord, master, and teacher gets down on his knees in front of his students and mentees and washes their dirty, smelly feet.

Note the timing: it's the night before he dies, in the middle of his final lecture covering really big topics, and at this meal through which the disciples will remember him for all time. Amazingly, this is when Jesus stops "talking the talk" and takes a knee, actually takes two knees to serve others. This action is so startling and "unacceptable" that impetuous Peter's first reaction is: "Never!" As in other places, I'm amused by Peter.

But it's Jesus washing Judas's feet that most blows my mind. By this time, the devil was already in Judas's heart, and Jesus must have known, and yet he washes Judas's feet. You're a better man than me, Jesus. But isn't this the whole point? Jesus, the great teacher, stops talking and shows us what we should do, even when our natural instincts go a different way. I, too, have to serve not only the good guys and my loyal friends but even my betrayers, enemies, nonfriends—*everyone*—in his name.

I have to get involved and help with smelly parts of people's lives. Probably not the feet, but there's a lot about all of us, including our spirit, emotions, attitudes, and behavior, that are not so clean and could use a good washing.

Jesus, you've given me an example, and told me to do it, but it's hard. Please cut me a little slack and give me a lot of help.

1 John 4:7–12, 20–21

Love of God, Love of Humankind

Beloved, let us love one another, because love is from God; everyone who loves is born of God and knows God. Whoever does not love does not know God, for God is love. God's love was revealed among us in this way: God sent his only Son into the world so that we might live through him. In this is love, not that we loved God but that he loved us and sent his Son to be the atoning sacrifice for our sins. Beloved, since God loved us so much, we also ought to love one another. No one has ever seen God; if we love one another, God lives in us, and his love is perfected in us.

Those who say, "I love God," and hate their brothers or sisters, are liars; for those who do not love a brother or sister whom they have seen, cannot love God whom they have not seen.

The commandment we have from him is this: those who love God must love their brothers and sisters also.

Ponderings

This aspect of the "love thing" is simple and in two parts:

1. Get the order right: God started it. He loved us first and showed it by sending Jesus to save us on the cross.
2. Connect the dots: No claiming to love God, the Divine One, without loving your brothers and sisters, the human ones.

If that's not enough, keep in mind the great act of God's love took place on a Friday afternoon on an agonizing and humiliating wooden cross. No flowers nor candy kisses! This "love thing" of the Bible may be easy to state but living it out is another story. Pretty clear...if you ask me! I guess we could opt out of loving one another if it's too hard—not my thing, doesn't suit my karma—but we then have to take the next step of admitting we do not love God. Seems harsh. OK, but don't blame the ponderer (*me*).

5

DON'T WASTE GOD'S TIME
(But Stay in Touch, No Matter What)

MATTHEW 6:7–13

How to Pray

When you are praying, do not heap up empty phrases as the Gentiles do; for they think that they will be heard because of their many words. Do not be like them, for your Father knows what you need before you ask him.

"Pray then in this way:
   Our Father in heaven,
hallowed be your name.
   Your kingdom come.
Your will be done,
   on earth as it is in heaven.
Give us this day our daily bread
   And forgive us our debts,
as we also have forgiven our debtors.
   And do not bring us to the time of trial,
but rescue us from the evil one."

Ponderings

I nominate these verses as the most repeated in the entire Bible. We call them "The Lord's Prayer" or "Our Father." We've taken "prayer license" in changing the words a bit in the standard version that we use, and some add a bit more at the end. Not to worry. All of us, whatever religion, should go over again Jesus's tips. All too often, I find myself rattling on, getting narcissistic and lecturing rather than listening to God.

Here's how I sum up Jesus's prayer tips:

1. Focus *first* on God—not yourself.
2. Think about God's kingdom and God's ways (will) and make those the model for life now on earth.
3. Today, ask God what you need—today. Stop worrying about tomorrow! See how new age-ish Jesus is: "the power of now" and "no day but today," and all that! But won't I be hungry tomorrow? Yes, without a doubt! When tomorrow becomes today, God will still be around—ask again!
4. If you want something for yourself, be ready to give it to someone else—in this case forgiveness.
5. Ask to be kept away from evil. There's more than enough to go around, and you need God's help to do this—today.
6. Keep it short; get to the point. You're busy. I'm Busy. God's busy. (The Our Father is less than seventy words. That's one tweet, including the Amen!)

But we're not stuck with only these seventy words. Jesus said, "Pray in this way. So, use your own words, but follow my lead!"

(P.S. If you want some tips for *each* verse of the Our Father, you'll find them in "A Closer Look" in Part 3.)

PSALM 13

When Abandoned

How long, O LORD? Will you forget me forever?
　　How long will you hide your face from me?
How long must I bear pain in my soul,
　　and have sorrow in my heart all day long?
How long shall my enemy be exalted over me?
　　Consider and answer me, O LORD my God!
Give light to my eyes, or I will sleep the sleep of
　　death,
　　and my enemy will say, "I have prevailed";
my foes will rejoice because I am shaken.
　　But I trusted in your steadfast love;
my heart shall rejoice in your salvation.
　　I will sing to the LORD,
because he has dealt bountifully with me.

Ponderings

Sometimes I have to remind God that I need him. Yeah, I know in my head he's always around, but somedays I'm not really feeling it. Maybe my faith is too weak, but some days "in the head" isn't enough. I've gotta feel it to keep going on the right track.

Especially when everybody is ganging up on me. God, I want to know whose side you're on. God, will you let "them" win? I want to trust in you, but please pick up the phone, answer my text—going to voicemail just isn't working for me. Please don't tempt me to go the route of a lot of folk who think they can do this spirituality thing on their own without you. You've got to answer me and show your face more. I'll make you a deal: if you help me, I will let everybody know how good you are. These days, even you can use more good PR and more friends. I'm in if you are.

PSALM 51:1–15

When Bad

Have mercy on me, O God,
　　according to your steadfast love;
according to your abundant mercy
　　blot out my transgressions.
Wash me thoroughly from my iniquity,
　　and cleanse me from my sin.

For I know my transgressions,
　　and my sin is ever before me.
Against you, you alone, have I sinned,
　　and done what is evil in your sight,
so that you are justified in your sentence
　　and blameless when you pass judgment.
Indeed, I was born guilty,
　　a sinner when my mother conceived me.

You desire truth in the inward being;
　　therefore teach me wisdom in my secret heart.
Purge me with hyssop, and I shall be clean;
　　wash me, and I shall be whiter than snow.
Let me hear joy and gladness;
　　let the bones that you have crushed rejoice.
Hide your face from my sins,
　　and blot out all my iniquities.

Create in me a clean heart, O God,
　　and put a new and right spirit within me.

Do not cast me away from your presence,
    and do not take your holy spirit from me.
Restore to me the joy of your salvation,
    and sustain in me a willing spirit.

Then I will teach transgressors your ways,
    and sinners will return to you.
Deliver me from bloodshed, O God,
    O God of my salvation,
and my tongue will sing aloud of your deliverance.

O Lord, open my lips,
    and my mouth will declare your praise.

Ponderings

If you're in a hurry, stop at verse 1: God, give me a dose of your mercy and autocorrect my moral typos, that is, vices and sins.

God's mercy is super-powerful in four ways: (1) it cleans me up, makes me rejoice; (2) it gives me spirit (the right one); and (3) it puts wisdom and truth deep down in me.

It so captivates me I must tell other sinners. (BTW: There are not many empty seats in this auditorium reserved for sinners, and my own seat is front and center.) I'm gonna tell these other sinners to stop running from you. Do not be afraid! You've got a big dose of mercy set aside for them, too.

It almost makes sinning worthwhile—not really, just joking.

But when I do sin again, as I'm sure I will, I'm "fessing up." God has another dose of his mercy for me.

PSALM 150

Whenever

Praise the LORD!
Praise God in his sanctuary;
   praise him in his mighty firmament!
Praise him for his mighty deeds;
   praise him according to his surpassing
      greatness!

Praise him with trumpet sound;
   praise him with lute and harp!
Praise him with tambourine and dance;
   praise him with strings and pipe!
Praise him with clanging cymbals;
   praise him with loud clashing cymbals!
Let everything that breathes praise the LORD!
Praise the LORD!

Ponderings

There is never a wrong time, place, or way to praise God. Whether sad or elated, just do it!

Do it everywhere, by whatever means, and with whomever.

Praise him by YouTube, text, and email.

Do it by Pandora, Vevo, and Spotify.

Do it by Facebook and Instagram. Praise God on cable and satellite.

Do it by iPhone and iPad, iOS, and Android.

When wireless and when hardwired, even in dead zones, praise the Lord!

Don't Waste God's Time

Do it with followers and friends.

Do it with posts, tweets, and blogs.

Do it by all those apps and new social media still to come.

Let everything and everyone be connected and say, "Praise!"

And one day, hopefully not too soon—in person, in his kingdom—praise the Lord!

6

THE BASICS OF THE BASICS
Death & Life

MATTHEW 27:1, 2, 11–14, 22–37, 45–54

The Crucifixion: A Sad, Unjust, Lethal Plot

A Silent King before Pilate (1, 2, 11–14)

When morning came, all the chief priests and the elders of the people conferred together against Jesus in order to bring about his death. They bound him, led him away, and handed him over to Pilate the governor.

Now Jesus stood before the governor; and the governor asked him, "Are you the King of the Jews?" Jesus said, "You say so." But when he was accused by the chief priests and elders, he did not answer. Then Pilate said to him, "Do you not hear how many accusations they make against you?" But he

44

gave him no answer, not even to a single charge, so that the governor was greatly amazed.

Pilate: A Profile in Courage—Not So Much (22-25)

Pilate said to them, "Then what should I do with Jesus who is called the Messiah?" All of them said, "Let him be crucified!" Then he asked, "Why, what evil has he done?" But they shouted all the more, "Let him be crucified!" So when Pilate saw that he could do nothing, but rather that a riot was beginning, he took some water and washed his hands before the crowd, saying, "I am innocent of this man's blood; see to it yourselves." Then the people as a whole answered, "His blood be on us and on our children!"

Stripped, Crowned, Mocked, Crucified (26-37)

So, he released Barabbas for them; and after flogging Jesus, he handed him over to be crucified.

Then the soldiers of the governor took Jesus into the governor's headquarters, and they gathered the whole cohort around him. They stripped him and put a scarlet robe on him, and after twisting some thorns into a crown, they put it on his head. They put a reed in his right hand and knelt before him and mocked him, saying, "Hail, King of the Jews!" They spat on him, and took the reed and struck him on the head. After mocking him, they stripped him of the robe and put his own clothes on him. Then they led him away to crucify him.

As they went out, they came upon a man from Cyrene named Simon; they compelled this man to carry his cross. And when they came to a place called Golgotha (which means Place of a Skull), they offered him wine to drink, mixed with gall; but when he tasted it, he would not drink it. And when they had crucified him, they divided his clothes among themselves by casting lots; then they sat down there and kept watch over him. Over his head they put the charge against him, which read, "This is Jesus, the King of the Jews."

Death (45–54)

From noon on, darkness came over the whole land until three in the afternoon. And about three o'clock Jesus cried with a loud voice, "*Eli, Eli, lema sabachthani*?" that is, "My God, my God, why have you forsaken me?" When some of the bystanders heard it, they said, "This man is calling for Elijah." At once one of them ran and got a sponge, filled it with sour wine, put it on a stick, and gave it to him to drink. But the others said, "Wait, let us see whether Elijah will come to save him." Then Jesus cried again with a loud voice and breathed his last. At that moment the curtain of the temple was torn in two, from top to bottom. The earth shook, and the rocks were split. The tombs also were opened, and many bodies of the saints who had fallen asleep were raised. After his resurrection they came out of the tombs and entered the holy city and appeared to many. Now when the centurion and those with him, who were keeping watch over Jesus, saw the earthquake and what took place, they were terrified and said, "Truly this man was God's Son!"

Ponderings

Here's the plot. (I get goosebumps every time I read this part of the Bible.)

A religious and political collusion forged from the zeal, jealousy, fear, and self-interest of religious and political leadership results in the suffering and public execution of Jesus, Son of God, son of Mary, on Calvary's hill in front of his own mother and a few friends. We know there's more, but let's not get ahead of ourselves. This is *it*! The cross of Jesus Christ is at the center of Christian faith. There is no salvation, no Christianity with the cross of Jesus. That's just the way it is. For those at the foot of the cross, they had every good reason to think this was the end of the story.

OK, a Spoiler Alert: This incredibly sad and patently unjust lethal conspiracy will backfire in less than seventy-two hours, on the third day. The Crucified One, dead and buried on Friday afternoon, will rise on Sunday morning. Through his suffering and death, all human suffering and deaths are to be transformed. In his rising to new life, all are offered new life. Tune into the next chapter!

MARK 16:1–14

Resurrection: Third Day, Empty Tomb, Confusion, Life

When the sabbath was over, Mary Magdalene, and Mary the mother of James, and Salome bought spices, so that they might go and anoint him. And very early on the first day of the week, when the sun had risen, they went to the tomb. They had been saying to one another, "Who will roll away the stone for us from the entrance to the tomb?" When they looked up, they saw that the stone, which was very large, had already been rolled back. As they entered the tomb, they saw a young man, dressed in a white robe, sitting on the right side; and they were alarmed. But he said to them, "Do not be alarmed; you are looking for Jesus of Nazareth, who was crucified. He has been raised; he is not here. Look, there is the place they laid him. But go, tell his disciples and Peter that he is going ahead of you to Galilee; there you will see him, just as he told you." So they went out and fled from the tomb, for terror and amazement had seized them; and they said nothing to anyone, for they were afraid. Now after he rose early on the first day of the week, he appeared first to Mary Magdalene, from whom he had cast out seven demons. She went out and told those who had been with him, while they were mourning and weeping. But when they heard that he was alive and had been seen by her, they would not believe it.

After this he appeared in another form to two of them, as they were walking into the country. And they went back and told the rest, but they did not believe them.

Later he appeared to the eleven themselves as they were sitting at the table; and he upbraided them for their lack of faith and stubbornness, because they had not believed those who saw him after he had risen.

Ponderings

Friday's lethal execution backfires on the religious and political conspirators! Jesus didn't stay dead as his enemies planned and his family and followers feared. This is really, really *it*! Without the empty tomb, I'm not writing this and you're not reading it.

Yet the women's early morning discovery wasn't very clear to them at the moment. They knew he was killed. They knew he was buried. They went to the tomb with spices expecting to find the body of dead Jesus. Can you blame them? The lack of belief and understanding doesn't end at the tomb. Others close to Jesus weren't sure. They mistrusted one another. Different followers met him in different places—on the road, in the garden, in the upper room—and it took them awhile to recognize him as alive again. Jesus even yelled at them for not believing!

Let's admit this is not an auspicious beginning to the greatest triumph of human history: the resurrection of Jesus (Jesus should really have hired a better advance team—I'm just saying...).

But here's a curious thought: maybe it's better the disciples didn't get it all then and maybe it's better we don't get it all now. Huh? Think about it: the resurrection of Jesus is too big, bold, good, and futuristic for our minds, hearts, and spirits to take it all in. It is the mind-blowing experience of all time! We need to always be a little confused, a little amazed, a little frightened by the reality that even death itself can't constrain and end God's love and life. But there's more, especially for those of us who like me have more than a bit of self-interest.

Can I really grasp that not only did Jesus rise from the dead, but I, too, am going to rise? And there's a very important bonus to this "resurrection thing." Because Jesus is already risen, I don't have to wait until death. I can get at least a half-portion of it here on earth. *Whew*—that's a lot to take in. Tell me more. Coming up next, in the Acts of the Apostles, the third member of Team God: the Holy Spirit!

7

THE NEW AGE
Team God Unleashes Its Spirit Member

Acts 2:1–4, 14–18, 22–32, 38–41

*The Spirit's Debut Attracts Huge
Crowds & Peter Preaches*

When the day of Pentecost had come, they were all together in one place. And suddenly from heaven there came a sound like the rush of a violent wind, and it filled the entire house where they were sitting. Divided tongues, as of fire, appeared among them, and a tongue rested on each of them. All of them were filled with the Holy Spirit and began to speak in other languages, as the Spirit gave them ability.

But Peter, standing with the eleven, raised his voice and addressed them, "Men of Judea and all who live in Jerusalem, let this be known to you, and listen to what I say. Indeed, these are not drunk, as you suppose, for it is only nine o'clock in the morning. No, this is what was spoken through the prophet Joel:

The New Age

'In the last days it will be, God declares,
that I will pour out my Spirit upon all flesh,
    and your sons and your daughters shall
        prophesy,
and your young men shall see visions,
    and your old men shall dream dreams.
Even upon my slaves, both men and women,
    in those days I will pour out my Spirit;
        and they shall prophesy.'"

"You that are Israelites, listen to what I have to say: Jesus of Nazareth, a man attested to you by God with deeds of power, wonders, and signs that God did through him among you, as you yourselves know—this man, handed over to you according to the definite plan and foreknowledge of God, you crucified and killed by the hands of those outside the law. But God raised him up, having freed him from death, because it was impossible for him to be held in its power. For David says concerning him,

'I saw the Lord always before me,
    for he is at my right hand so that I will not be
        shaken;
therefore my heart was glad, and my tongue
        rejoiced;
    moreover my flesh will live in hope.
For you will not abandon my soul to Hades,
    or let your Holy One experience corruption.
You have made known to me the ways of life;
    you will make me full of gladness with your
        presence.'

"Fellow Israelites, I may say to you confidently of our ancestor David that he both died and was buried, and his tomb is with us to this day. Since he was a prophet, he knew that God had sworn with an oath to him that he would put one of his descendants on his throne. Foreseeing this, David spoke of the resurrection of the Messiah, saying,

'He was not abandoned to Hades,
nor did his flesh experience corruption.'

This Jesus God raised up, and of that all of us are witnesses."

Peter said to them, "Repent, and be baptized every one of you in the name of Jesus Christ so that your sins may be forgiven; and you will receive the gift of the Holy Spirit. For the promise is for you, for your children, and for all who are far away, everyone whom the Lord our God calls to him." And he testified with many other arguments and exhorted them, saying, "Save yourselves from this corrupt generation." So those who welcomed his message were baptized, and that day about three thousand persons were added.

Ponderings

New Age, Third Age, whatever you want to call it, is one of the big moments in God's dealing with us human folk. I know the Spirit's debut on Pentecost doesn't have the appeal and following of the Baby Jesus's debut in the manger at Bethlehem. (Does anything?) It's not up there with the Father's leading role in Creation and Adam and Eve in the Garden of Eden with its much better imagery, but this moment is a really, really Big Deal: this is our story, our moment, our age—then in the first century, *now* in the twenty-first century, and in all the centuries until—who knows when...he comes again.

We weren't there for Creation and we didn't get to walk naked in the garden. We didn't cross the Red Sea and enter the promised land. We didn't get to see Jesus in the flesh, but we do get his Spirit—just as he promised. I'm thinking maybe it's better we have the Spirit member of Team God with us for our entire life for billions of us for centuries and centuries. No offense, Jesus, but you only hung out on earth for a few years with a small number—pretty exclusive. Glad that Dad and you sent your Spirit to carry on for all of us! (I'm just saying.)

There's a lot of theatrics to the Spirit's debut at Pentecost on center stage, Jerusalem: fiery tongues, a mighty wind, tongue-tied followers now speaking multiple languages, prophesies, visions, people from afar, mass conversions, and baptisms. (Marketing crew was much better than for the resurrection!) Not quite Bruce Springsteen, Lady Gaga, Stevie Wonder, Beyoncé, or Prince at the Super Bowl, but still an impressive performance. Jerusalem must have been quite a scene that day: a huge revival meeting with magic-like flares and pyrotechnics.

Once the stage is set in a big way, Peter makes a bold pitch. The elevator speech edition goes like this: Jesus is of good stock, David's line, sent by our God as anointed Messiah. Some bad guys killed him, but God raised him up from the dead. He's alive and offers forgiveness, salvation, and the gift of the Holy Spirit. You're in if you repent and are baptized in the name of Jesus. That's the deal!

How'd Peter do?

- **Day 1**: 3,000 took the deal
- **Days 2 through 10**: many more were added

- **Day 723,065**: 1.6 billion Christians today (give or take)

Pretty impressive, but I guess what really matters is not then, but now, and not 1.6 billion, but me and you. I guess I have time because the Spirit will be around until Jesus comes again. But I probably shouldn't wait. Why lose out on the Spirit's wisdom and strength for today by waiting until tomorrow. How do I let this ubiquitous divine "holy" Spirit into my not-so-holy human spirit? Just ask! Once I do, how do I listen to the Spirit's whisperings? Just shut up (sorry, not polite), be quiet, and listen.

1 CORINTHIANS 12:3–13

One Spirit, but Different Gifts for Different Folks

Therefore, I want you to understand that no one speaking by the Spirit of God ever says "Let Jesus be cursed!" and no one can say "Jesus is Lord" except by the Holy Spirit.

Now there are varieties of gifts, but the same Spirit; and there are varieties of services, but the same Lord; and there are varieties of activities, but it is the same God who activates all of them in everyone. To each is given the manifestation of the Spirit for the common good. To one is given through the Spirit the utterance of wisdom, and to another the utterance of knowledge according to the same Spirit, to another faith by the same Spirit, to another gifts of healing by the one Spirit, to another the working of miracles, to another prophecy, to another the discernment of spirits, to another various kinds of tongues, to another the interpretation of tongues. All these are activated by one and the same Spirit, who allots to each one individually just as the Spirit chooses.

For just as the body is one and has many members, and all the members of the body, though many, are one body, so it is with Christ. For in the one Spirit we were all baptized into one body—Jews or Greeks, slaves or free—and we were all made to drink of one Spirit.

Ponderings

The Spirit is quite a talented member of Team God. Seems Jesus chose a great advocate and counselor for his followers on earth after he went back to heaven. Thanks.

The Spirit has a large toolkit of gifts, customized for different followers. No cookie cutter one-size-fits-all here! That's good for us humans because I'm me, not you; and you're you, not me. We each get our own gift. We're a big family, all made in God's image, but that image shows up in so many wonderful (for the most part) varied ways. God treats us as individuals. I like that. I bet you do, too.

I can't figure out how the Spirit decides who gets what. (That's one of my questions for heaven.) One gets wisdom, another greater faith, a third can do great works. Some interpret and discern, some preach, and some heal. But these different gifts and many more are from the same Spirit. Even though there are such differences, together we are one in Jesus.

Really? Nice inspiring words, but is that what I experience all, or even most, of the time? Unity (uniformity?) and diversity (divisiveness?) are challenges (problems?) humankind has faced since the Garden of Eden and the Tower of Babel.

WHAT'S THE MESSAGE?

Even Jesus didn't solve them when he was here. Remember, even he used the Samaritan–Jewish antipathy to make a point.

Now in our "enlightened" twenty-first century we have our own chasm-like divides: race, religion, nationality, class, ideologies, politics—some very, very ugly. Certain language and attitudes, even among us Christians, require great leaps of faith to see the one Spirit of God drawing us into one body in Christ.

Spirit, I like your platform, but you've been around for over two thousand years. When are you going to deliver on it? It's the Age of the Spirit, but disunity is still a problem, taking even greater tolls on the poor and vulnerable. I mean no disrespect. I'll help, but your power is much greater. Please step it up!

8

FOOD FOR THE EARTHLY JOURNEY
His Body & Blood

MATTHEW 26:26–29 & LUKE 22:19

The Last Supper in Jerusalem

While they were eating, Jesus took a loaf of bread, and after blessing it he broke it, gave it to the disciples, and said, "Take, eat; this is my body." Then he took a cup, and after giving thanks he gave it to them, saying, "Drink from it, all of you; for this is my blood of the covenant, which is poured out for many for the forgiveness of sins. I tell you, I will never again drink of this fruit of the vine until that day when I drink it new with you in my Father's kingdom."

Then he took a loaf of bread, and when he had given thanks, he broke it and gave it to them, saying, "This is my body, which is given for you. Do this in remembrance of me."

Ponderings

For Catholic Christians, communion, the Eucharist, the Mass is the central act of our common worship and prayer to God.* We trace its roots to this Last Supper scene of Jesus with his disciples. Give me a shot at distilling this into a more contemporary language.

Jesus arranges a meal for his closest colleagues and tells them, "I'm going away, but this meal is my perpetual gift to you. Keep sharing a meal together like we are doing tonight, and I'll be there. I know this may be hard to understand, but when you eat this bread and drink this wine, you will actually be sharing my own body and blood. Do this and you will be part of the saving mystery of everything that will happen in the next few days."

I doubt they understood all the "theology" embedded in Jesus's mandate. I doubt they had much of an inkling of what was about transpire in the new covenant of his blood. But, as the Bible records, they did what their friend and teacher asked and received a very stupendous farewell gift that keeps giving until Jesus comes back.

1 CORINTHIANS 11:23–26

A Feisty Bunch of Christians

> For I received from the Lord what I also handed on
> to you, that the Lord Jesus on the night when he

---

* Communion is also very important for many but not all other Christians. If this were a theological treatise, we'd go into the deep and complex understanding of this great mystery. By now, you're not expecting this, and so we won't. There is plenty of material elsewhere to look up.

was betrayed took a loaf of bread, and when he had given thanks, he broke it and said, "This is my body that is for you. Do this in remembrance of me." In the same way he took the cup also, after supper, saying, "This cup is the new covenant in my blood. Do this, as often as you drink it, in remembrance of me." For as often as you eat this bread and drink the cup, you proclaim the Lord's death until he comes.

Ponderings

And so it goes with his memorial meal: Paul received it and passed it on to the feisty Corinthians, and they passed it on, and so it goes until today.

It is this meal of remembrance in which Jesus is present through the bread and wine of communion that is celebrated weekly today by hundreds of millions of people on every continent throughout the world.

Two key ideas: remembrance and presence—much richer and more connected than their ordinary usage. Remembrance includes making present, not merely looking back. Presence includes participation and active engagement in what is being remembered. Jesus is present through "remembering" what he did on the night before he died. By eating this bread and drinking this cup, we are part of the covenant of Jesus's death and resurrection. The new covenant—death, yes—no avoiding it. But after death: life! Jesus is really present, not nostalgically as a memory, but as the living risen Lord. Even now that's hard to fully get all at once. That's why we do it again and again. There's more to understand, appreciate, be nourished by, and rejoice in.

9

LENIENCY ON THE WAY
Not So Much at the End

MATTHEW 13:24–30
Weeds & Wheat Together

[Jesus] put before them another parable: "The kingdom of heaven may be compared to someone who sowed good seed in his field; but while everybody was asleep, an enemy came and sowed weeds among the wheat, and then went away. So when the plants came up and bore grain, then the weeds appeared as well. And the slaves of the householder came and said to him, 'Master, did you not sow good seed in your field? Where, then, did these weeds come from?' He answered, 'An enemy has done this.' The slaves said to him, 'Then do you want us to go and gather them?' But he replied, 'No; for in gathering the weeds you would uproot the wheat along with them. Let both of them grow together until the harvest; and at harvest time I will tell the reapers,

Collect the weeds first and bind them in bundles to be burned, but gather the wheat into my barn.'"

Ponderings

"Don't throw the baby out with the bathwater!" Isn't Jesus just giving us a variation on this well-known saying? Yes, I guess so, but some days I'm on the side of the servants. Why wait? It would be great to rid the world of all those bad people and things right now! Can't we find "better gardeners" or a precision laser strike that surgically distinguishes weeds from wheat? Doesn't Jesus have a sharp eye? I'm just saying.

But then I get it. Sometimes the enemy who sows problematic weeds into my life—is actually me. As they say, "I'm my own worst enemy." Is that sometimes true for you, too? Neither is it all one way or the other. Aren't there weeds and wheat within each of us? As we stumble along, it's hard to line up all the saints on one side of the street and the sinners on the other. (Hold on a moment! Wait for the next passage about the endgame with Jesus.)

Each day, we see things and we actually do things that are magnificent, good, and holy, and, on the same day, we see and do things that fall on the other side of the ledger. The weeds and wheat are entangled outside and inside me. So I have to admit, if the gardeners are rooting out evil today, some pretty big spades are coming my way

God, thank you for calling them to stand down on this rooting out till the end. It gives me some time to do my self-rooting-out. While you and I are waiting, God, please help me live my best (or better) self. I need your help. Thanks.

Luke 13:6–9
One More Chance

Then [Jesus] told this parable: "A man had a fig tree planted in his vineyard; and he came looking for fruit on it and found none. So he said to the gardener, 'See here! For three years I have come looking for fruit on this fig tree, and still I find none. Cut it down! Why should it be wasting the soil?' He replied, 'Sir, let it alone for one more year, until I dig around it and put manure on it. If it bears fruit next year, well and good; but if not, you can cut it down.'"

Ponderings

Two thoughts:

First, God is more patient than I am (frankly, not a very high bar...just saying). I would have torn down the fig tree the first year it didn't produce. And now, God's extending it to a fourth-year grace period. God is pretty generous with fig trees. But the beauty of all this parable-speak of Jesus is parables are about more than the image used— in this case the fig tree. They're really about you and me. *Gracias a Dios*, because I don't care much about fig trees (yes, not nice, but true). But I do care about you and me. And so, God gives you and me grace periods, and I need them— probably more than four. How about you?

Second, I find the reason the fig tree is being put on probation telling. The poor tree didn't do anything wrong. It just did nothing. It didn't hurt anybody. Maybe it was wasting a little soil. It just didn't produce. How often do we religious types, when accused of whatever, say, "I didn't do anything" and "I didn't do anything wrong"? We'd be better off taking "the Fifth." Aren't we condemning ourselves with our words? Like the fig tree, if all I'm doing is taking up space and wasting time, shouldn't I be on probation?

God, please send me a kind gardener, or two, with the right type of fertilizer. I've already got too much of the wrong type. If you do that, I promise to try to do my part. I know I shouldn't be negotiating with you, but you did let Father Abraham bargain with you on Sodom and Gomorrah. Deal?

Matthew 25:31–46

The Final Exam

"When the Son of Man comes in his glory, and all the angels with him, then he will sit on the throne of his glory. All the nations will be gathered before him, and he will separate people one from another as a shepherd separates the sheep from the goats, and he will put the sheep at his right hand and the goats at the left. Then the king will say to those at his right hand, 'Come, you that are blessed by my Father, inherit the kingdom prepared for you from the foundation of the world; for I was hungry and you gave me food, I was thirsty and you gave me something to drink, I was a stranger and you welcomed me, I was naked and you gave me clothing, I was sick and you took care of me, I was in prison and you visited me.' Then the righteous will answer him, 'Lord, when was it that we saw you hungry and gave you food, or thirsty and gave you something to drink? And when was it that we saw you a stranger and welcomed you, or naked and gave you clothing? And when was it that we saw you sick or in prison and visited you?' And the king will answer them, 'Truly I tell you, just as you did it to one of the least of these who are members of my family, you did it to me.' Then he will say to those at his left hand, 'You that are accursed, depart from me into the eternal fire prepared for the devil and his angels; for I was hungry and you gave me no food, I was thirsty and you gave me nothing to drink, I was a stranger and you did not welcome me, naked and you did not give me clothing, sick and in prison and you did not visit me.' Then they also will answer, 'Lord, when was it that we saw you hungry or thirsty or a stranger or naked or sick or in prison, and did not take care of you?' Then he will answer them, 'Truly I tell you, just as you did not do it to one of the least of these, you did not do it to me.' And these will go away into eternal punishment, but the righteous into eternal life."

Ponderings

(This one's longer, but it's pretty important—like final exams, I've got lots of thoughts about it. By now you know the rules—skip this if it is too much for you and just read the Bible passage.)

Oops...what happened to good, kind, sweet, patient Jesus? He tossed some jalapeños into his message. Eternal life (*YES!*) an option, along with (*GULP*) eternal punishment! More to the message than "I'm OK; you're OK."

Leniency on the Way

In my college classes, often the first probing intellectual questions each semester were: "What's on the final exam?" followed by "How will I be graded?"

Here's Master Teacher Jesus's answer for his students (followers—you and me). The final exam is about the course-work of your life; it's "pass–fail," and these are the life-experience questions:

1. Did you feed a hungry person? (Sharing hors d'oeuvres at a cocktail party doesn't count.)
2. Did you give something to drink to a thirsty person? (Water to marathon runners gets you partial credit.)
3. Did you welcome the stranger? (How did you do when "one of them" moved nearby?)
4. Did you give clothes to a naked person? (Good marks if you took the time to bring old clothes to the thrift store—extra credit if some new sweaters were among them. Bad marks if you just threw them out because the thrift store wouldn't pick them up on *your* schedule.)
5. Did you care for a sick person? (Both family and friends count; extra credit if they're crabby!)
6. Did you visit someone imprisoned? (Not a stroll in the park, but among the greatest acts of human solidarity. That's why it's a question on Jesus's final exam.)

Thanks, Jesus. This is helpful. It's straightforward and you've given us a lifetime. I get your point. If I say holy things about you and your father, and if the Spirit makes me praise aloud, I have to do good things for the people around me. Not always easy to fulfill, but you're pretty clear on what you expect of your followers.

WHAT'S THE MESSAGE?

But wait a minute...there's nothing on the final exam about sex, going to church, stealing, lying, and all those other things religious types have been telling us for years are important. How can this be? Maybe Matthew left things out. The "Big" Bible and even my attention-challenged basic version has some of these. Let's go back to the college classroom again. There's more to the course than the final exam. So there's a lot more to faith, religion, and spirituality than the last judgment. There's a lot of good and important guidance not on the final exam. Let's not disregard it. But, between you and me, I'm concentrating on the final exam.

10

LET'S GET TO THE END
...Not Really

Revelation 21:1–7, 19–27

A New Heaven & a New Earth

Then I saw a new heaven and a new earth; for the first heaven and the first earth had passed away, and the sea was no more. And I saw the holy city, the new Jerusalem, coming down out of heaven from God, prepared as a bride adorned for her husband. And I heard a loud voice from the throne saying,

"See, the home of God is among mortals.
He will dwell with them;
they will be his peoples,
and God himself will be with them;
he will wipe every tear from their eyes.
Death will be no more;
mourning and crying and pain will be no more,
for the first things have passed away."

And the one who was seated on the throne said, "See, I am making all things new." Also, he said, "Write this, for these words are trustworthy and true." Then he said to me, "It is done! I am the Alpha and the Omega, the beginning and the end. To the thirsty I will give water as a gift from the spring of the water of life. Those who conquer will inherit these things, and I will be their God and they will be my children."

The foundations of the wall of the city are adorned with every jewel; the first was jasper, the second sapphire, the third agate, the fourth emerald, the fifth onyx, the sixth carnelian, the seventh chrysolite, the eighth beryl, the ninth topaz, the tenth chrysoprase, the eleventh jacinth, the twelfth amethyst. And the twelve gates are twelve pearls, each of the gates is a single pearl, and the street of the city is pure gold, transparent as glass.

I saw no temple in the city, for its temple is the Lord God the Almighty and the Lamb. And the city has no need of sun or moon to shine on it, for the glory of God is its light, and its lamp is the Lamb. The nations will walk by its light, and the kings of the earth will bring their glory into it. Its gates will never be shut by day—and there will be no night there. People will bring into it the glory and the honor of the nations. But nothing unclean will enter it, nor anyone who practices abomination or falsehood, but only those who are written in the Lamb's book of life.

Ponderings

How's this for a great ending that's not an ending at all? The often-glib phrase about one door closing and another opening actually is true, and what a new door it is. The current old order—tears, death, pain—is kaput. All things are being transformed and made new.

The new Jerusalem with its magnificent inspiring image is worth coupling with that of the current Jerusalem. I've been to Jerusalem twice and seen the holy sites of all three major religions sharing the same space with armed guards, fear, and insecurity. It's paradoxical that the current city of Jerusalem, the very name of which signifies peace, is hallowed by all three great Abrahamic religions, also appears as a shameful symbol of religious intolerance, hatred, and violence. See how these Christians, Muslims, and Jews love one another—*really*?

Sorry for the downer; back to the good stuff:

A new Jerusalem, a new "Everyland," is coming, where God himself is the light that guides and welcomes the glory of the nations through its wide-open gates. It's the hot (oops, *cool*) vacation spot—for all eternity!

Free, life-giving water for the thirsty! Hint: That's shorthand for all kinds of good free stuff to delight and fulfill us. (BTW: I'm betting the water is a tap or well, not a pretentious designer-bottled variety.) Here in the new heaven and new earth God gives each of us free gifts and abundance to meet our individual needs: to hungry people, food; to those who are homeless, homes; to lonely people, friends; to oppressed people, justice; to folks who are isolated, camaraderie; to those who are rejected, acceptance; to sinners, mercy; to saints, halos; to strangers, welcome; to people who are sick, health; to the devil, a pitchfork (just kidding, and giving the devil his due); to those who are anxious, peace. Add your own gift to the list!

To each person, God gives faith, hope, and love—the greatest of these—forever. I can't wait...well, maybe I can wait a little while longer. *Halleluiah!* Amen.

PART 2

BONUS PASSAGES

11

FINDING GOD'S WORD

DEUTERONOMY 30:11–20

Read Your Own Heart, Follow It, and Live!

Surely, this commandment that I am commanding you today is not too hard for you, nor is it too far away. It is not in heaven, that you should say, "Who will go up to heaven for us, and get it for us so that we may hear it and observe it?" Neither is it beyond the sea, that you should say, "Who will cross to the other side of the sea for us, and get it for us so that we may hear it and observe it?" No, the word is very near to you; it is in your mouth and in your heart for you to observe.

See, I have set before you today life and prosperity, death and adversity. If you obey the commandments of the LORD your God that I am commanding you today, by loving the LORD your God, walking in his ways, and observing his commandments, decrees, and ordinances, then you shall live and become numerous, and the LORD your God will bless you in the land that you are entering to possess. But if your heart turns away and you do not hear, but are led astray to bow down to other gods and serve them, I declare to you today that you shall perish; you shall not live long in the land that you are crossing the Jordan to enter and possess. I call heaven and earth to witness against you today that I have set before you life and death, blessings and curses. Choose life so that you and your descendants may live, loving the LORD your God, obeying him, and holding fast to him; for that means life to you and length of days, so that you may live in the land that the LORD swore to give to your ancestors, to Abraham, to Isaac, and to Jacob.

Ponderings

Pretty straightforward, if you ask me! Looking for God's commands is not a scavenger hunt in the skies above or across the ocean blue. They're right under our nose—actually, within our very own human heart. The commands are not externally imposed; they emerge from within. It sounds like New Age "fulfilling human potential" to me! OK, but who made the human heart...and in his own image and likeness, so he knows what we will find there? God knows the stark choices that face us: (A) Walk in God's ways, and the path leads to abundant blessing and living, or (B) Don't, and we're heading toward evil and dying. It seems Father-God can be a tough negotiator.

Maybe the simplest summary: Listen to your heart, follow the natural obvious choice you'll find there, and you will live the good life; or else: New age spirituality with a touch of the Godfather, brought to you by Moses from the ancient desert. Who would've thunk it?

12

GOD GETS ANGRY WHEN HIS PEOPLE MESS UP

Jeremiah 5:1–30

Watch Out!

Run to and fro through the streets of Jerusalem,
   look around and take note!
Search its squares and see
   if you can find one person
who acts justly
   and seeks truth—
so that I may pardon Jerusalem.
Although they say, "As the Lord lives,"
   yet they swear falsely.
O Lord, do your eyes not look for truth?
You have struck them,
   but they felt no anguish;
you have consumed them,
   but they refused to take correction.

WHAT'S THE MESSAGE?

They have made their faces harder than rock;
   they have refused to turn back.

Then I said, "These are only the poor,
   they have no sense;
for they do not know the way of the LORD,
   the law of their God.
Let me go to the rich
   and speak to them;
surely they know the way of the LORD,
   the law of their God."
But they all alike had broken the yoke,
   they had burst the bonds.

Therefore a lion from the forest shall kill them,
   a wolf from the desert shall destroy them.
A leopard is watching against their cities;
   everyone who goes out of them shall be torn in
       pieces—
because their transgressions are many,
   their apostasies are great.

How can I pardon you?
   Your children have forsaken me,
   and have sworn by those who are no gods.
When I fed them to the full,
   they committed adultery
   and trooped to the houses of prostitutes.
They were well-fed lusty stallions,
   each neighing for his neighbor's wife.
Shall I not punish them for these things?
     says the Lord;
   and shall I not bring retribution
   on a nation such as this?

God Gets Angry when His People Mess Up

Go up through her vine-rows and destroy,
    but do not make a full end;
strip away her branches,
    for they are not the LORD's.
For the house of Israel and the house of Judah
    have been utterly faithless to me,
        says the Lord.
They have spoken falsely of the LORD,
    and have said, "He will do nothing.
No evil will come upon us,
    and we shall not see sword or famine."
The prophets are nothing but wind,
    for the word is not in them.
Thus shall it be done to them!

Therefore thus says the LORD, the God of hosts:
Because they have spoken this word,
I am now making my words in your mouth a
        fire,
    and this people wood, and the fire shall devour
        them.
I am going to bring upon you
    a nation from far away, O house of Israel,
        says the LORD.
It is an enduring nation,
    it is an ancient nation,
a nation whose language you do not know,
    nor can you understand what they say.
Their quiver is like an open tomb;
    all of them are mighty warriors.
They shall eat up your harvest and your food;
    they shall eat up your sons and your daughters;
they shall eat up your flocks and your herds;
    they shall eat up your vines and your fig trees;

they shall destroy with the sword
   your fortified cities in which you trust.

But even in those days, says the LORD, I will not make a full end of you. And when your people say, "Why has the LORD our God done all these things to us?" you shall say to them, "As you have forsaken me and served foreign gods in your land, so you shall serve strangers in a land that is not yours."

Declare this in the house of Jacob,
   proclaim it in Judah:
Hear this, O foolish and senseless people,
   who have eyes, but do not see,
   who have ears, but do not hear.
Do you not fear me? says the LORD;
   Do you not tremble before me?
I placed the sand as a boundary for the sea,
   a perpetual barrier that it cannot pass;
though the waves toss, they cannot prevail,
   though they roar, they cannot pass over it.
But this people has a stubborn and rebellious
     heart;
   they have turned aside and gone away.
They do not say in their hearts,
   "Let us fear the LORD our God,
who gives the rain in its season,
   the autumn rain and the spring rain,
and keeps for us
   the weeks appointed for the harvest."
Your iniquities have turned these away,
   and your sins have deprived you of good.
For scoundrels are found among my people;
   they take over the goods of others.

Like fowlers they set a trap;
  they catch human beings.
Like a cage full of birds,
  their houses are full of treachery;
therefore they have become great and rich,
  they have grown fat and sleek.
They know no limits in deeds of wickedness;
  they do not judge with justice
the cause of the orphan, to make it prosper,
  and they do not defend the rights of the needy.
Shall I not punish them for these things?
      says the LORD,
  and shall I not bring retribution
  on a nation such as this?

An appalling and horrible thing
  has happened in the land.

Ponderings

God is really sounding off to his "chosen people." Apparently, they're not acting too "chosen." Even the "great ones" have acted badly. The people rebelled: have a stubborn heart, act treacherously...God goes on and on. It seems he could easily indict and convict on multiple counts of "unfaithfulness."

Watch out! God's not going for "time served." Foreigners will take you over. Your food, animals, and plants—even your children—will be devoured. If you missed the point: "Don't get God angry!"

Then what? God refused to close the deal: he won't "completely" end them. As furious as God can be, he still keeps them as his chosen, special people. *Really*? They are unfaithful and he is faithful. He might be angry, yes, and punishing, yes, but *always* faithful!

But I am relieved because I need as many chances as I can get. I know it's not a free pass; God wants us to act in certain ways and the threat of his wrath looms. (Consult with those people of Jeremiah's time.) Who can figure this God out? Could it be because he has put his image within us?

13

A NEW DEAL: WHERE?

JEREMIAH 31:1, 13, 31–34

In Everybody's Heart

At that time, says the LORD, I will be the God of all the families of Israel, and they shall be my people.

Then shall the young women rejoice in the dance,
    and the young men and the old shall be merry.
I will turn their mourning into joy,
    I will comfort them, and give them gladness for
      sorrow.

The days are surely coming, says the LORD, when I will make a new covenant with the house of Israel and the house of Judah. It will not be like the covenant that I made with their ancestors when I took them by the hand to bring them out of the land of Egypt—a covenant that they broke, though I was their husband, says the LORD. But this is the covenant that I will make with the house of Israel after those days, says the LORD: I will put my law within them, and I will write it on their hearts; and I will be their God, and they shall be my people. No longer shall they teach one another, or say to each other, "Know the LORD," for they shall all know me, from the least of them to the greatest, says the LORD; for I will forgive their iniquity, and remember their sin no more.

Ponderings

Jeremiah's "new covenant" turns some usual notions on their head about religion, religious leaders, and God. I guess that's in a prophet's job description!

I'm getting a little nervous. It seems Jeremiah (speaking for God) may have caught on to us "professional" religious types. Sometimes we make religion complicated and God seem too far away. And worse, religious leaders all too often try to make themselves God's gatekeepers! God can take care of himself—thank you very much!

God himself writes what he wants from us on our hearts. God's doing the forgiving—direct access. God & us: He's our Guy; we're his peeps. I like that.

14

AN END TO THE WEARINESS

Isaiah 40:1–5, 9–11, 29–31

Take Comfort

Comfort, O comfort my people,
    says your God.
Speak tenderly to Jerusalem,
    and cry to her
that she has served her term,
    that her penalty is paid,
that she has received from the Lord's hand
    double for all her sins.

A voice cries out:
"In the wilderness prepare the way of the Lord,
    make straight in the desert a highway for our
        God.
Every valley shall be lifted up,
    and every mountain and hill be made low;

WHAT'S THE MESSAGE?

the uneven ground shall become level,
    and the rough places a plain.
Then the glory of the LORD shall be revealed,
    and all people shall see it together,
    for the mouth of the LORD has spoken."

Get you up to a high mountain,
    O Zion, herald of good tidings;
lift up your voice with strength,
    O Jerusalem, herald of good tidings,
    lift it up, do not fear;
say to the cities of Judah,
    "Here is your God!"
See, the Lord GOD comes with might,
    and his arm rules for him;
his reward is with him,
    and his recompense before him.
He will feed his flock like a shepherd;
    he will gather the lambs in his arms,
and carry them in his bosom,
    and gently lead the mother sheep.

He gives power to the faint,
    and strengthens the powerless.
Even youths will faint and be weary,
    and the young will fall exhausted;
but those who wait for the LORD shall renew their
      strength,
    they shall mount up with wings like eagles,
they shall run and not be weary,
    they shall walk and not faint.

Ponderings

God's spiritual comfort food is how I think of these verses. It's not mac & cheese, but spiritually it doesn't get much better. You can take these verses straight or hear them in your head from the opening of Handel's *Messiah*: Comfort ye! Comfort ye!

God's promise: comfort, guilt ended, no more hairpin turns, the potholes are filled, no delays on the commute, strength when I'm weak, courage when I'm faint, stick-to-it-ness for the long haul, fly above it all (well, maybe not that, but one can hope).

Tell the good news on high! Take comfort—and the mac & cheese too!

Reread the verses and relax: God's got your back!

15

A NON-MAJESTIC MESSIAH

Isaiah 53:2–12

Spurned and Suffering

For he grew up before him like a young plant,
   and like a root out of dry ground;
he had no form or majesty that we should look at him,
   nothing in his appearance that we should desire
      him.
He was despised and rejected by others;
   a man of suffering and acquainted with
      infirmity;
and as one from whom others hide their faces
   he was despised, and we held him of no account.

Surely he has borne our infirmities
   and carried our diseases;
yet we accounted him stricken,
   struck down by God, and afflicted.

A Non-Majestic Messiah

But he was wounded for our transgressions,
     crushed for our iniquities;
upon him was the punishment that made us
          whole,
     and by his bruises we are healed.
All we like sheep have gone astray;
     we have all turned to our own way,
and the LORD has laid on him
     the iniquity of us all.

He was oppressed, and he was afflicted,
     yet he did not open his mouth;
like a lamb that is led to the slaughter,
          and like a sheep that before its shearers is silent,
     so he did not open his mouth.
By a perversion of justice he was taken away.
     Who could have imagined his future?
For he was cut off from the land of the living,
     stricken for the transgression of my people.
They made his grave with the wicked
     and his tomb with the rich,
although he had done no violence,
     and there was no deceit in his mouth.

Yet it was the will of the LORD to crush him with
          pain.
When you make his life an offering for sin,
     he shall see his offspring, and shall prolong his
          days;
through him the will of the LORD shall prosper.
     Out of his anguish he shall see light;
he shall find satisfaction through his knowledge.
     The righteous one, my servant, shall make many
          righteous,

and he shall bear their iniquities.
Therefore I will allot him a portion with the great,
    and he shall divide the spoil with the strong;
because he poured out himself to death,
    and was numbered with the transgressors;
yet he bore the sin of many,
    and made intercession for the transgressors.

Ponderings

Isaiah never met Jesus—obviously. But with twenty-twenty hindsight, we Christians can say Isaiah nailed it (oops, no pun intended) about Jesus's suffering and death on the cross to save the world.

This is not a pretty picture of the way God saves us. Yes, God's servant (Jesus) shall win, accomplish God's will, justify many, see the light, intercede for sinners. But, what a price: suffering, pain, being spurned, seized, crushed, no esteem. Jesus takes on our sins in pain, suffering, and death and heals us, makes us whole and saves us. Why did God do it this way? I don't know. Couldn't there have been an easier way? There must have been, but this is the way God chose. (Another question for heaven!)

The pain and suffering in our time—racial injustice, a worldwide pandemic, political divisiveness, inequities in wealth, and so many others—make these verses even more poignant and necessary. His suffering is our hope because he took on all our suffering and pain and enables them to be transformed.

I'm glad Jesus did this for me, but please don't ask me to explain it all—I can't. This passage is harsh. No comfort food here.

16

GOD'S TURNAROUND PLAN FOR THE DOWNTRODDEN

Isaiah 61:1–8

Justice

The spirit of the Lord GOD is upon me,
  because the LORD has anointed me;
he has sent me to bring good news to the oppressed,
  to bind up the brokenhearted,
to proclaim liberty to the captives,
  and release to the prisoners;
to proclaim the year of the LORD's favor,
  and the day of vengeance of our God;
  to comfort all who mourn;
to provide for those who mourn in Zion—
  to give them a garland instead of ashes,
the oil of gladness instead of mourning,
  the mantle of praise instead of a faint spirit.

They will be called oaks of righteousness,
the planting of the LORD, to display his glory.
They shall build up the ancient ruins,
they shall raise up the former devastations;
they shall repair the ruined cities,
the devastations of many generations.

Strangers shall stand and feed your flocks,
foreigners shall till your land and dress your
vines;
but you shall be called priests of the LORD,
you shall be named ministers of our God;
you shall enjoy the wealth of the nations,
and in their riches you shall glory.
Because their shame was double,
and dishonor was proclaimed as their lot,
therefore they shall possess a double portion;
everlasting joy shall be theirs.

For I the LORD love justice,
I hate robbery and wrongdoing;
I will faithfully give them their recompense,
and I will make an everlasting covenant with
them.

Ponderings

Now here's a God you want to believe in. Good news:
God is on the side of the underdogs and society's outcasts—
those who are afflicted and brokenhearted, with prisoners
and mourners. Even ruined cities he restores. But even better,
God not only speaks sympathetically but he has the juice to
turn things around. (Is it rude to ask, "*When*"?)

God's Turnaround Plan for the Downtrodden

But don't miss God's motivation for this transforma-
tion: "For God loves justice." There are complicated ways to
talk about justice. I like to keep it simple. Every person gets
at least a sufficient share of what is needed. It's OK by me if
some people have more, as long as everybody has enough of
the basics to live with dignity. I know we are a long, long way
from there. Our world is filled with so much injustice so that
billions of people don't have what they need, such as enough
food, a decent place to live, a good job, a loving family, access
to health care, to name a few basics. Besides physical lack,
so many are afflicted, brokenhearted, displaced, and captive.
(If you want to check out basic human needs and rights, see
either the United Nations' "Universal Declaration of Human
Rights" [1948] or Pope John XXIII's *Encyclical Pacem in Terris*
[1963]. The list is pretty much the same.)

I am glad God has justice on his agenda, but I risk imper-
tinence and wish that God would give this a higher priority. I
know, "in his kingdom." But I still don't understand why God
doesn't do things in my time frame.

17

GOD'S GOT YOUR BACK

LUKE 12:22–32

Forget Fretting—It Won't Help

He said to his disciples, "Therefore I tell you, do not worry about your life, what you will eat, or about your body, what you will wear. For life is more than food, and the body more than clothing. Consider the ravens: they neither sow nor reap, they have neither storehouse nor barn, and yet God feeds them. Of how much more value are you than the birds! And can any of you by worrying add a single hour to your span of life? If then you are not able to do so small a thing as that, why do you worry about the rest? Consider the lilies, how they grow: they neither toil nor spin; yet I tell you, even Solomon in all his glory was not clothed like one of these. But if God so clothes the grass of the field, which is alive today and tomorrow is thrown into the oven, how much more will he clothe you—you of little faith! And do not keep striving for what you are to eat and what you are to drink, and do not keep worrying. For it is the nations of the world that strive after all these things, and your Father knows that you need them. Instead, strive for his kingdom, and these things will be given to you as well.

"Do not be afraid, little flock, for it is your Father's good pleasure to give you the kingdom."

Ponderings

This is the tree hugger's dream and the compulsive's nightmare. No offense meant to either group! I am not a psychologist, so these superficial pop opinions come easy.

Compulsives need focus and control, obviously a fool's task, but it does occupy many people's time and energy, especially someone who is trying to squeeze the essence of the whole Big Book into a very short volume. I plead guilty!

So, I'm supposed to just trust God, pay attention to his kingdom, live for today. What about next month's rent or mortgage payment? You think tuition costs are going down? How secure is my job? How about a relationship I'm in: where will it be next year or three years from now? This is tough for many of us—letting go.

Isn't there something that I can do? Yes! Seek God's kingdom and you get the whole enchilada, without worry. OK, but it's fuzzy if you ask me.

This is a strong antidote for the way many of us live our lives: anxiety about things we cannot control and over-reliance on our own ability and cleverness. We often couple this with too little focus on God's graciousness and love, and the promise of his kingdom.

I get it. I even agree. But for us compulsives, loving our enemy is a piece of cake compared with this version of "letting go and letting God."

18

FATHER, NOT ME!

Matthew 26:36–39

What Faithfulness Requires

Then Jesus went with them to a place called Geth-semane; and he said to his disciples, "Sit here while I go over there and pray." He took with him Peter and the two sons of Zebedee, and began to be grieved and agitated. Then he said to them, "I am deeply grieved, even to death; remain here, and stay awake with me." And going a little farther, he threw himself on the ground and prayed, "My Father, if it is possible, let this cup pass from me; yet not what I want but what you want."

Ponderings

Let's get this straight: Jesus was no masochist! He was truly human, alive, and aware of what was going on, and he hated the prospect of pain and suffering—like the rest of us. He knew what crucifixion meant and he wanted out, but he was a good son. He knew the mission the Father had given him, and if this was what it took, then he would do it.

We Christians need to pay attention. Unfortunately, some people say the "true" way to be Christian is to look for ways to suffer so we can be united with Jesus's passion and death. Two points: First, no need to look for suffering; it will find us soon enough. There's plenty to go around. Second, there's no problem with trying to avoid or alleviate suffering for others and ourselves. The exception to this is we have to accept and endure suffering to be faithful to God's wisdom and way. Parents sometimes must endure suffering and sacrifice, and even put themselves in danger to be good parents. A businessperson has to be honest even when they have to sacrifice an important deal. One doesn't seek these situations, but faithfulness demands enduring the hurt—in order to remain faithful.

19

ALL YOU NEED IS LOVE

JOHN 13:31–35

The Christian Brand

When he had gone out, Jesus said, "Now the Son of Man has been glorified, and God has been glorified in him. If God has been glorified in him, God will also glorify him in himself and will glorify him at once. Little children, I am with you only a little longer. You will look for me; and as I said to the Jews so now I say to you, "Where I am going, you cannot come." I give you a new commandment, that you love one another. Just as I have loved you, you also should love one another. By this everyone will know that you are my disciples, if you have love for one another."

Ponderings

Can you match the brand identifier with the company?	
ARCH	Nike
LOVE	McDonald's
SWOOSH	Christian Louboutin
RED BOTTOMS	Apple
ONE-BITE	Christian

On the night before he died, Jesus gave his disciples their brand identifier: LOVE—the Jesus way. Sadly, I fear this two-thousand-year-old brand may be less identified in the lives of the Christians than the swooshes, arches, red bottoms, and one-bites of their respective products. We have work to do—and a lot of it.

One challenge is making sure we strive for "Jesus-love" with the cross at the center. Christian love puts the good of others before my own comfort and convenience. Even when it's not an ultimate sacrifice, Jesus-love means smaller sacrifices of serving and helping others, even washing smelly feet.

Fortunately, so many have done this brand of love proud. Most of them we don't know and have never heard of. Some we call saints. They give us a model and inspiration. Yet, realistically, we must admit that many who claim Jesus's brand have some work to do to faithfully represent Jesus-love in the world.

20

GOING BACK TO HEAVEN & GOODBYE

LUKE 24:50–53 & ACTS 1:13

Not So Fast

Then he led them out as far as Bethany, and, lifting up his hands, he blessed them. While he was blessing them, he withdrew from them and was carried up into heaven. And they worshiped him, and returned to Jerusalem with great joy; and they were continually in the temple blessing God.

When they had entered the city, they went to the room upstairs where they were staying.

Ponderings

All good things must end! It's been a whirlwind thirty-some-odd years or so. Jesus is born on earth; he grows and lives; he teaches; he dies (executed, to be precise); he rises and now returns to heaven. Goodbye—sort of...but there's more to come. The disciples head back to Jerusalem: a little praise, joy, blessing in the temple, but most of all waiting, waiting in the upper room for—what God has in store for them next.

Maybe that's a good tip for us two thousand years later: a little praise, joy, and blessing and waiting—being open to God's spirit of wisdom and counsel.

21

GO, BAPTIZE, AND TEACH

Matthew 28:16–20

"I'll Be There," He Said

Now the eleven disciples went to Galilee, to the mountain to which Jesus had directed them. When they saw him, they worshiped him; but some doubted. And Jesus came and said to them, "All authority in heaven and on earth has been given to me. Go therefore and make disciples of all nations, baptizing them in the name of the Father and of the Son and of the Holy Spirit, and teaching them to obey everything that I have commanded you. And remember, I am with you always, to the end of the age."

Ponderings

A daunting parting assignment is given by the Big Boss of heaven and earth: (1) Go everywhere, (2) Recruit, (3) Baptize,

(4) Teach Everything. How is it possible for this small band of bunglers? Ah, Jesus will be around to help—*always*! That's how. And the third member of Team God will be coming on the scene. So, Team God's member two exits the earthly scene to make way for Team God's member three, and the Holy Spirit's spectacular ushering in of a whole new era on Pentecost.

22

NOT FOR WEDDINGS

1 Corinthians 12:31 & 13:1–13

For Life!

But strive for the greater gifts. And I will show you a still more excellent way.

If I speak in the tongues of mortals and of angels, but do not have love, I am a noisy gong or a clanging cymbal. And if I have prophetic powers, and understand all mysteries and all knowledge, and if I have all faith, so as to remove mountains, but do not have love, I am nothing. If I give away all my possessions, and if I hand over my body so that I may boast, but do not have love, I gain nothing.

Love is patient; love is kind; love is not envious or boastful or arrogant or rude. It does not insist on its own way; it is not irritable or resentful; it does not rejoice in wrongdoing, but rejoices in the truth. It bears all things, believes all things, hopes all things, endures all things.

Love never ends. But as for prophecies, they will come to an end; as for tongues, they will cease; as for knowledge, it will come to an end. For we know only in part, and we prophesy only in part; but when the complete comes, the partial will come to an end. When I was a child, I spoke like a child, I thought like a child, I reasoned like a child; when I became an adult, I put an end to childish ways. For now we see in a mirror, dimly, but then we will see face to face. Now I know only in part; then I will know fully, even as I have been fully known. And now faith, hope, and love abide, these three; and the greatest of these is love.

Ponderings

Do you think Paul composed this text for a wedding ceremony at Corinth? Probably not, but I hope he gets royalties for every time it's read at a wedding. Enough distraction...

For me, these verses are a most magnificent "Ode for the Common Christian"—a way of life prescribed and accessible, and a call for every person. This list roots Christian love in daily living: being patient, kind, and truthful, not rude, nor quick-tempered. I know what Paul's tips mean and I know we all can do them—or, like me, so often fall short in trying. They suit every part of daily lives: work, play, family, relationships. These "routine" things are actually much more important than some of the flashy stuff: prophecy, martyrdom, speaking in tongues, moving mountains in prayer. (Although at least once, I'd like to move a mountain!)

And let's not forget, love is the greatest. When in doubt: love. I can't think of a situation in which love is the wrong choice.

PART 3

TWO OLDIES

(Too Goodie to Be Left Out)

23

THE LORD IS MY SHEPHERD

PSALM 23

Guaranteed

The Lord is my shepherd, I shall not want.
> But I do want…

He makes me lie down in green pastures;
> My pastures are gray: asphalt and concrete, the
> inside of a car, and too many restless nights
> that leave me unrefreshed in the morning.

he leads me beside still waters;
> Yes, I am calmed by the ocean, lakes, and rivers if
> I can ever get to them.

he restores my soul.
> He does, but not often enough…

He leads me in right paths
> But I don't always follow. I stray down idle ways.

for his name's sake.
> Sometimes I try to make a name for myself.

WHAT'S THE MESSAGE?

Even though I walk through the darkest valley,
> Some places are truly dark and it's not just my
> paranoia.

I fear no evil;
for you are with me;
> But I do fear, evil—and many other things. Be
> with me in my worries and anxiety.

your rod and your staff—
they comfort me.
> I like that you are powerful and can protect me.
> Some days I just want you to beat up a few
> people for me! Come on, please just do it!
> And I'll be brave—or at least try to be…

You prepare a table before me
> I like the great things you give. Good eats!

in the presence of my enemies;
> Yes, I admit it: it's good my enemies know you're
> on my side.
> Nice but…my God's bigger and better than their
> God.

you anoint my head with oil;
> Your soothing oil is even better than my mousse
> or warpaint.

my cup overflows.
> I like "super-sized" portions of your blessings.

Surely goodness and mercy shall follow me
> When I look over my shoulder, I'm not so sure;
> I see a few other things, but I can hope and
> dream…

all the days of my life,
> I like lifetime guarantees!

and I shall dwell in the house of the LORD
> Now there's a housing plan!

my whole life long.
> No rent increases, with utilities and amenities
> included; a no-interest mortgage, and
> evergreen for all eternity. The Lord is my
> Shepherd.

24

THE OUR FATHER

Matthew 6:9–13

A Closer Look

Our Father
> Think of the good that human fathers do—
> And multiply that for our heavenly Father
> Think of the bad that human fathers do—
> Think of the opposite;
> That's what our heavenly Father does.
> But don't stop there, God's not limited by human
>   gender traits;
> So, think of the good that human mothers do—
> And multiply that for our heavenly Mother
> Think of the bad that human mothers do—
> Think of the opposite;
> That's what our heavenly Mother does.

who art in heaven,
> Sometimes you are distant, and I am mad and
>   frustrated.
> Sometimes you are distant, and I am glad.

The Our Father

Sometimes it's just right.

When we talk in that space, beyond earth's noise
and chaos, I can hear whispers of heaven's
peace and happiness.

That's nice!

hallowed be thy name;

Your name and your very being:

Hallowed, holy, whole, awesome.

My name and my very being—not so much:

Hollow, profane, fractured, trembling—

Wait!

Didn't you make me in your likeness?

May your hallowedness fill my hollowness;

your wholeness heal my fractures;

your awesomeness calm my trembling.

Holy, Holy, Holy…

thy kingdom come.

I usually pray for my kingdoms and their toys
and riches.

Your kingdom I usually refer to as heaven, and
after I die—very distant.

But if I think of your kingdom's riches: peace, joy,
happiness, justice,

I could use them here and now.

Your kingdom…*your* kingdom come! Mine can
wait a bit!

Thy will be done

Two problems with this one:

I want to do my will…

But OK, I have to admit—you're God and so
your will trumps,

Even if I'm stubborn and don't like it.

What is your will? Is today "tough love" or "ten-
der kindness" day?

WHAT'S THE MESSAGE?

Your son Jesus had both kinds of days:

Whips for the money changers in the temple;
    mercy for the woman caught in adultery.

So, Father, with my family, friends, and co-
    workers: What is your will?

Don't be shy….Speak up! Let me know and I'll
    try…

on earth, as it is in heaven.

Earth, my hood; Heaven, your hood

Your hood's far away and perfect. Mine's in my
    face and flawed.

I want my earth to be like your heaven—and I
    don't want to wait until I die.

So, when you walk with me on my earthly
    journey—as you promised!—

Don't come empty-handed; bring heaven's gifts;

But I warn you: Me and my people are going to
    want to steal them.

I'm counting on you sharing them—at least a bit.

Give us this day our daily bread,

Today's prayer for today's needs!

Jesus extolled "the power of now"—long before
    contemporary gurus.

No accruals from yesterday. No deferrals for
    tomorrow.

Pretty sly of you, God! You know how to keep
    your power base.

Tomorrow, you'll make me ask again.

But you know my distractions and impatience
    when you don't answer right away and my inse-
    curity that you won't be there again tomorrow…

So, I have an idea. Suppose I make one big prayer
    for the month—kind of like paying my bills…
    um—I don't see you nodding yes.

The Our Father

Then please help me to trust your way and turn
to you anew each day.
Give me the bread that fulfills my hopes and
heals my hurts—today.
I'll be back tomorrow!

**and forgive us our trespasses, as we forgive
those who trespass against us;**

I like the word *trespass*—a neat, grown-up word
for mess-ups,
And nonthreatening, even better!
Kinda like a kid crossing a neighbor's property to
chase a ball.
Other words scare me: *evil, sin, cruelty, selfish-
ness.*
God, as long as we keep this between us, I'll cop
to you some of those bad things.
I'll take the deal. It seems fair.
Forgive my mess-ups and I'll forgive those who
messed me up, if I have to.
But I'm gonna need your help to close my side of
the bargain.
And BTW, one final thing:
Could you help me to forgive myself?
Sometimes that's really hard.
Thanks.

and lead us not into temptation,

Really!
You're such a Debbie Downer.
Temptations can be exciting. Sometimes it's fun
to play with fire.
Do you want me to be boring?
Didn't Jesus hang out with sinners?
By now you reckoned I'm more arguing than
praying this one.

WHAT'S THE MESSAGE?

You put me in the world, and you told it to light
up its darkness and shadows.
But isn't that where temptation lurks?
I think I get it. I'm weak and can't resist some
bad things.
So, it's better to not be led there.
But I'm pretty sure it's not so simple or…
Maybe I just disagree.
Do you really only want me to play it safe?
We have to talk more about this one!

but deliver us from evil.

Please keep me out of evil's way:
The everyday personal sins,
Like acting mean and selfish,
Cheating, not helping a friend, and a lot of other
things.
But, Father, there's more—
I'm not only asking for me, but for all of us.
And "all of us" together have some big devils
stalking us
That we need to be rid of:
Violence, famine, inequality, abject poverty, rac-
ism, pandemics, many "isms."
Big guy! How about some deliverance here?
Hope I'm not being disrespectful, but…
God, you gotta do a better job on some of these
biggies!

**For thine is the kingdom, and the power and
the glory, forever and ever.**

Go, God!
Peace, happiness, fulfillment, and understanding
are yours,
When and where they show up.
Your Son and his kingdom tag along—even now.

The Our Father

Remember, I prayed at the beginning: "Thy king-
    dom come"?
Help me calm down (not easy) and
be drawn peacefully (harder still)
into the mystery of your kingdom's power and
    glory—
here and now on earth.
You made me; you saved me; you love me.
Let me bask in your power and glory forever,
But *now* too.
AMEN.
So be it.
I'll be quiet and rest in your peace.
If you have something to say:
A whisper or a shout; a sound bite or a text…
Just let me know.

ABOUT THE AUTHOR
What Kind of Person Would Write Bible Basics?

Kevin Sullivan has read and studied the Bible for decades, thinks it's the most important book ever written, and sees no contradiction in believing that we don't have to spend a lot of time poring over every verse to get at "the Big Book's" basics: God's creative and saving love for all humanity—openly offered to each of us.

You would never guess Kevin Sullivan was a priest, or a monsignor for that matter, if you met him away from his "churchy" haunts. Most people know Kevin (aka Monsignor) from one of the many other professional hats he wears. He is the truest definition of a Gemini: a mixture of paradoxes. Kevin is deeply spiritual and irreverently obsessed with the light and dark of secular culture and social media. He stanchly holds that self-help and God's help are essential in the quest for success, fulfillment, and happiness.

He epitomizes the yin and yang of everything. His calendar is the proof! An Israeli high school near Gaza and Iraqi refugee camps near Mosul have been on his itinerary. Meeting garment workers in Bangladesh and attending black-tie galas are marked for the same week. Comforting the sick in hospitals and visiting prisoners segue into challenging politicians over flawed public policies.

If you happen to meet him at his day gig as CEO of Catholic Charities of the Archdiocese of New York, you might not hear him curse like a sailor, but you would see his dedication to helping "the least among us." If you caught him in rare form hosting his own weekly Sirius radio talk show or guesting on Jenny McCarthy's, you would swear he was the most liberal conservative you had ever heard. If you sat in on a graduate class he taught at New York University or Notre Dame, or if you heard him preach on Sunday, or at the funeral of a stock exchange president or grass roots community activist, you would bet money he thinks that far too much of the whole organized religion thing is a sham. But he's playing the game like a true baller, mining and sharing the golden nuggets Jesus left us. He believes heavenly hope and earthly cynicism are perfect strategic partners in making the world a better place.

At the spry age of seventy, he's been there and done (most of) that:

- Woodstock ✓
- Parish priest ✓
- 9/11 ✓
- Popes (including Francis) and presidents ✓
- Country estates and county jails ✓
- Beyoncé, Rod Stewart, and Pink concerts ✓
- Writer, preacher, blogger, executive, listener ✓✓✓✓

Above all, Kevin is human. He has loved and been loved. He laughs and cries easily. He only accepts what rings true to him about religion (including the Bible), politics, friends, life's "shoulds," and most everything that constrains us mere mortals. In all his gigs, he listens and talks. Kevin listens well—most of the time. What he talks about are authentic hopes, dreams, insecurities, and fears that strike a chord with many of us human folk.